Teen

real teens

Diary of a
Junior Year

volume 4

SCHOLASTIC INC.
New York Toronto London Auckland Sydney
Mexico City New Delhi Hong Kong

ISBN 0-439-08411-3

Distributed under license from
The Petersen Publishing Company, L.L.C.
Copyright © 1999 The Petersen Publishing
Company, L.L.C. All rights reserved.
Published by Scholastic Inc.

 Produced by 17th Street Productions,
a division of Daniel Weiss Associates, Inc.
33 West 17th Street, New York, NY 10011

 Teen is a trademark of Petersen
Publishing Company, L.L.C.

SCHOLASTIC and associated logos are trademarks and/or registered trademarks of Scholastic Inc.

12 11 10 9 8 7 6 5 4 3 2 1   0 1 2 3 4/0 5/0

Printed in the U.S.A.   01
First Scholastic Printing, January 2000

The photograph used on this cover was taken by a real teenager in Eastside High School in Gainesville, Florida. The subjects pictured are real students but they are in no way associated with the real teens in this book.

Special Thanks to Laura Dower

Diary of a Junior Year

volume 4

The diaries you are about to read are real. Names, places, and other details have been changed to protect the teens involved. But what they have to say all really happened.

Marybeth Miller:

I'm a wiseass. I can make just about anyone smile, even if they're feeling down in the dumps, and that's really important 2 me. Some days I consider myself fatter than others, but what are you gonna do, right? I run track and play basketball and keep on—so it's no big deal. Mostly I love just hanging out with my friends. Mom, Dad, and my brother and sister r cool 2, I guess. I mean, we don't <u>always</u> get along, but I pull thru. I don't think I would want anything else.

    <u>LIKES:</u> My yellow Polo shirt

    <u>DISLIKES:</u> People who can't take a joke

Billy Shim:

I'm an outgoing, crazy guy, but I have mixed feelings about it. I'm smart and get good grades, but I know that's not good enough so I need something that stands out like sports, sports, sports! The scene with my parents is totally up/down. We have great moments, but we have arguments too—like good grades = heaven and

2

bad grades = hell. But my older brother Lee, who's playing football at college right now, he's always there for me. Lee is the nicest guy you could ever meet. I think things would be easier if I were more like him.

    <u>LIKES</u>: Sports, sports, sports (esp. lacrosse in spring)

    <u>DISLIKES</u>: Stupid, clingy chicks

<u>Teresa Falcone:</u>
    There is much more going on in my mind than the eye can see . . . I love writing, reading, dancing, singing, acting, playing field hockey, listening to all kinds of music, and most of all being with my friends and family. I know I'm smart and get really good grades, but I have this problem, which is everyone sees me as this airhead. I hate that! Sometimes I can be sooooo insecure! My parents are divorced, so I live with my mom and my older brother Vincent, even though we don't get along ever. My dad lives a town away, so I see him a lot

<u>LIKES</u>: Romance books and anything else romantic!

<u>DISLIKES</u>: Not being taken seriously!

Jake Barosso:

Ladies think I'm cute, but only sometimes. I'm shy, but I love to dance and I'm always on the go. I love raving, riding a Jet Ski, playing pool, and fixing up my new car. My dad is really really sick, so things are terrible at home right now, but I try to help out as much as I can. We're always arguing about the stupidest things. I wish it didn't have to be like this. I like to make Mom + sis laugh whenever I can. I'm funny too.

<u>LIKES</u>: My car!!!

<u>DISLIKES</u>: Being sick + people who are assholes (a tie)

Katie Carson:

I am involved in Community Club and student council, on the tennis team, and a peer ministry leader of my church, among other things. To fit it all into one word, I am well-rounded. My schedule is nuts, but I handle stress with my sense of humor. I have important long-term goals for myself. Sometimes my friends tell me I am naive about things, but I really do believe I have the ability to get along with everyone. The most important thing to me is family— we're very close and share a special bond. I can tell my mom everything.

LIKES: Musical theater, travel, good grades, Brad

DISLIKES: People who don't have any goals

Edward Baxter:

This is me. I'm all the characteristics associated with this picture. I love listening to music, watching TV, and playing Nintendo. I'm a yearbook editor, sometimes I run track and I'm in Community Club, even though I'm starting to hate it, and I mean REALLY HATE IT. I'm also a bad speller, but for the most part I do well in school. As far as parents go, mine

are like big kids. My dad is a real comedian and my mom is
stupid funny, like me. My older brother Jerry is away at college.

<u>LIKES</u>: Coconut my dog

<u>DISLIKES</u>: People who never call you back, especially
when you beep them

<u>Emma West</u>:

I think I'm totally trustworthy, kind,
and respectful, but if someone starts
talking about me behind my back I feel a
lot different and I get upset. At school
I'm ice-hockey manager and I'm in
community club and student council. I
love hanging out but I usually don't make
any plans until like the last minute,
usually with marybeth. The most important
thing is that my friends mean the world
to me. my parents are cool too. They're
always running around doing a million
different things and my little brother
Ronnie thinks he runs the house. my
sister Lynn and I have to babysit for him

6

a lot, which can be a drag but whatever.
   <u>LIKES</u>: Having a boyfriend
   <u>DISLIKES</u>: Being left out

Kevin Moran

   I'm all this: smart, funny, hyper, and I don't know what else kind of guy. I kinda go from one thing to another like wave running, clubbing, swimming, mainly any sport—and mostly just chilling with my friends. Still, I get bored all the time. My family, they're loud, and Dad has been married 2x so we have a lotta freakin people here to deal with and we argue like ALL THE TIME but that's cool I guess cuz I really do love them all. I was really close to my sis Lena, but she died like 8 years ago when I was 8, which still makes me mad.
   <u>LIKES</u>: Dressing and doing stuff exactly as I want it and no one can tell me anything else
   <u>DISLIKES</u>: My brother Neil no doubt!

Marybeth

January 7th

Guess who I talked to *again* last night? Big Paulie Wohl. Jeez is he hot! I can't stop thinking about him. What a way to start the new year 4 sure. He has really nice arms.

I also gave my number to this other guy that Emma told me about. This boy's a BB player named TJ. I dunno if he'll call tho. He said he would by the end of the weekend . . . we'll see. Three days to wait. I hope he does!!! I have this feeling that maybe TJ is just messing w/me. Emma says he def. likes me but who knows.

Oh by the way I haven't talked to Matt in like forever. Yeah, I thought Matt was gonna work out into something special like maybe friends w/benefits. But we have totally lost touch.

AND I TOTALLY DON'T CARE!

Kevin

1/7

This week is just flying by, and actually all of junior year is flying by, and still I am so tired b/c so far back to school is exactly the same & schoolwork sux yes as usual I can't stand it. I'm soo sick of this. I had a chem lab and of course that was bad b/c Mr. MacTaggart won't lay off, especially those of us who are having a tougher time than others understanding what is going on these days. Oh yeah, later on I tried to go to the freakin weight room & that was pretty much of a joke b/c when I was there the power squad was also there. They were fucking around w/jump ropes pretending to be all like dominatrix and S&M slaves and like whatever other weird shit they could think of. It was sooo funny Lazlo & Jake & I just couldn't stop laughing. And um well nothing else happening except maybe something w/me and Cristina maybe. I know we had that huge blowup a week or so ago about driving and all that around the new year but now we're talking a lot more and we both know that we like each other so we'll see what's going on. We'll just wait a little while to chill. Ta ta

Teresa

Jan 7
Dear Diary,   ↑ sign!!!

A romantic situation will develop.

So tonight I was flipping through the newspaper and I came across this picture & clipping about this star hockey player from a few towns away in Redwood. He plays for the Redwood Reds and his name is

Lawrence Gillooly and let me just tell you—he is *GOR-GEOUS*! I think I would make the perfect partner with him totally. Okay, his last name is Irish and I'm Italian, but together we'd be awesome. I know it. Here is this clipping about him. I put the picture up on my mirror.

LAWRENCE GILLOOLY, Reds

The 6-foot, 190-pound all-region champ returns to the Redwood Reds' front line after recording 33 goals and 19 assists last winter. Gillooly, who is also known as Gill, is extremely hard to knock off the puck. He is also fast on the ice, with enough speed to give the opposing defensive line a constant challenge.

The newspaper also said that he has a game this coming Saturday at an ice-hockey arena nearby and well . . . you can only guess where I'm gonna be on Sat.! Yeah—to his game! Plus I went online to see if I could find out what his team number is so I can watch out for him and what I discovered is that his # is 11. I almost died! That's *my* number in field hockey! That's incredible, I think. We have *SOOOOO* much in common—

Teresa (me)	Lawrence
Loves ice hockey*	Plays ice hockey
#11 on her team	#11 on his team
Junior in HS	Also a junior
* and I play *field* hockey!	

I think we may be *PERFECT* for each other. Now I just have to meet him. After all, I never did connect w/that Leonardo hockey guy—and he even knew my name (I think). Well, we'll see what happens. I just have this weird feeling in the pit of my stomach that Lawrence & I are meant to be together and that I am totally the woman for him. Is that so strange? I'm destined to meet him.

Oh my God, I have to go watch *Dawson's Creek* now! I know I say I hate that show sometimes, but other times it is so right about teens and love and all that. Bye!

Baxter

January 7

Here's something really strange. I got all uptight and worried about my physics test for *NOTHING*. Yes, I got a B and so basically I was wasting my time worrying for nothing. I feel like I do a lot of that lately, wasting time.

Lately I've been feeling like an outsider a little bit too. When Billy said that stuff to me the other night about being selfish I really took it personally. I don't think he has any idea how much what he says bugs me. He doesn't know. And he doesn't ever try to know or to ask me.

Everyone has someone special in their life who they're talking to or getting together with but me. I was on the phone tonight with Emma. All she can talk about is Cliff and I'm sick of it. I mean I'm happy for her but enough already. I wish I could have with Megan what Cliff and Emma have.

Emma

It's after 10 at night and I am so tired of talking to Cliff. We're fighting about stupid shit. I'm a little upset because he got a job and he works from Tuesday through to Saturday from like 5 to 11. And we had plans supposedly on Friday to go out but now we can't because he's working again. I mean, I know I can't be mad at him, but now we won't get to be together that much and that just upsets me a lot. The only day we can even hang out is Sunday, and usually I don't hang out with people then. Sundays are for lying around and just doing homework.

I dunno what to do about anything. Like, I wanna be mad but then Cliff goes and says the cutest things to me. Like today, he beeped me before he went to work with 822-143. That's his birthday date plus 143, which means "I love you." I was so excited to see that because he's never beeped me with that before.

I guess maybe I just have to deal with the hours on his job and see him Sundays or something. I mean, he wants to buy a car and that's why he needs money and a job. I guess it's important. I just have to stop missing him so much. He says he'll try to make more time for me.

Jake

More of time just dragging by. Still waking up every day and going to school like always, come home, eat, go to work, come home around 9:30 and do homework, and then watch reruns of *Friends* on TV. I could write the same thing in here every day if I wanted. That's how predictable life feels. And then in the middle of all that people are dying and being sick but I just keep on.

Yesterday I got even more, 4 more leads at the mortgage company. And yes, it snowed again today. I wanted to get out of school but we didn't. Me and Kevin went over to see Katie's dad again like last week, and he paid us to snowblow his driveway. He gave us way more money than he should have. I didn't even want him to pay, but that didn't work. Then me and Kevin had a snowball fight and acted stupid. It was fun I guess. My uncle is coming over for dinner later.

Katie

January 8
@ 5:50 P.M.

It snowed again tonight! Kevin and Jake came by and snowblowed our driveway, like they usually do. We played in the snow a little. We said we'd go out later, but it's really too icy to go *anywhere*.

All I can really say is, "Thank God it's Friday!" I can't even gauge how long this week seemed—it lasted forever, but yielded decent results. Life is pretty good. I got elected to this special committee for Community Club. I am really proud of that accomplishment. And of course, rehearsals have started for *The Boy Friend,* which should turn out well. We had a good one last night—except for Rachel's part. She is so self-absorbed. I know she's talented, but I can't believe the part she got.

As long as the stress load is constant, I am confident that I can exceed everyone's expectations of me for the rest of the year. I'm just going to keep moving along thanks to such a supportive family and friends.

Brad said he'd come over later so I'm just hanging out waiting for him. He's renting *Armageddon* again. We've already seen it once but we actually both like it—that *never* happens! He doesn't mind if it's icy out because he has 4-wheel drive on his Jeep. I can't wait for him to get here. He always makes me laugh my troubles away. I have so much going on!

History outline —take-home test essay
English —must read the last episode of Huckleberry Finn
Chem —need to reread p380 & work on my lab
Spanish —questions still need to be finished!
Don't forget to do work on Intrastate Committee

Billy

I just can't get into school. I don't want vacation to be gone. I don't want to deal with the snow or ice or any of it. My dad says he's worried about me taking the car b/c of the weather, which really pisses me off. But I guess it's true I've been caught speeding a lot so he assumes I'll get in some kind of accident or something.

But all that means is that I'm just stuck here at home doing nothing on Friday. No one called tonight to go anywhere. My mom wants me to help them out around the house and the store this weekend, which I am totally against but I haven't got anything else to do really. They run this small market so sometimes I work the register if they need me, like over the summer. But only sometimes. My parents know both Lee and I hate doing it so they don't ask much.

Just called Benjamin & Deke and no one was home. I think they're going to play ice hockey tomorrow. Just goofing around. This kind of sucks when it's just business as usual, day in day out, same old thing. I'm bored.

My Routine My Routine

Kevin:

During the week it's go 2 it wake up And shave And take a shower And put on moisturizer And cologne b/c I love that Tommy Hilfiger And then go get my car And pick up Jake And go to school And go to classes And spend some time just hangin w/my friends like Cristina And Lazlo And of course Jake we have a lot of fun together And then during the weekend it's sleep 4 me.

Teresa:

6:45 A.M.: My annoying alarm goes off and I hit it off angrily (I'm not a morning person)

7:00-7:45 A.M.: Breakfast, putting on makeup, doing my hair, getting dressed

8:00-8:15 A.M.: Downtime before school starts, mingle w/random people

8:20-9:05 A.M.: 1st period = gym/basketball. I hate sweating a lot in the morning —yuck!

My Routine My Routine

9:05-10:12 a.m.: 2nd period = history and as always I'm ready to fall asleep!

10:12-11:00 a.m.: 3rd period = Spanish w/the nicest, sweetest teacher in the whole world even though she can be soooo boring

11:00-11:47 a.m.: 4th period = English, which is my absolute favorite w/Miss Gifford! Right now we're reading A Farewell to Arms, by Hemingway, and I love that book. Now this class wakes me up!

11:50-12:20 P.m.: Lunchtime = I am totally starving!

12:20-1:10 P.m.: 5th period = math

1:10-2:00 P.m.: 6th period = SAT review class

2:00-2:45 P.m.: 7th period = physics, which is AWFUL. I hate it so much just like everyone else! I just sit there and stare at the clock and count down the minutes until the end of the day. And of course I have no idea what I am doing! Oh well.

2:50-3:00 P.m.: My bus ride home

3:00-8:00 P.m.: A lot of times I

17

take naps now when I get home
and then I wake up & then I eat
dinner and watch TV of course.
Then I get around to starting my
homework and usually I end up in
bed sometime like midnight or so!

Billy:

What is my routine? Wake up, drive, school,
sports (winter = football and spring = lacrosse)
and then homework so I can do well. Sometimes
I'm in chorus or the play, like this year I'm in The
Boy Friend. I also go to parties and have a good
time for a change. It's better when my parents
aren't in my face about doing my schoolwork. I
can get more done then.

Marybeth:

From day 2 day my routine will change
depending on what I am doing and if I feel
like doing n e thing different like
sometimes I will go 4 a long run or maybe
hang out w/Sher & Emma or some other
peeps!

My Routine My Routine

Baxter:

    6:00 wake up to radio
    7:00 drive my mother to the gym
    8:00 go to my locker and get books
    9:00 in classes all day
    12:00 eat turkey & lettuce sandwich or something
else for lunch
    3:00 leave school
    4:00 play Nintendo with my brother if he's home or
Derek
    5:00 eat dinner
    6:00 watch Comedy Central
    7:00 watch Friends
    8:00 take a short nap
    9:00 study
    10:00 read or write in my journal
    11:00 talk on the phone
    12:00 go to bed

My Routine My Routine

Emma:

Ok at 7:00 I get up and take a shower and then I get dressed, eat my breakfast, brush my teeth, dry my hair, put on my makeup and jewelry, and watch the end of MTV. Then I leave for school around 8:00 and go to Italian class and algebra and all my other classes and stand around with friends and go to my locker and space out when I am bored. Ok then at 2:48 I usually go home with Baxter. Then I have the rest of my day until like 11:00 when I go to bed after talking to Cliff of course.

Jake:

I go to school, I go to work, and I go to bed. Sometimes I can hang out but mostly I'm just working, especially since I have no girl. I will spend time with my dad if he's up to it. Or I'm with Kevin, usually partying over the weekend or whenever we can.

My Routine My Routine

Katie:

　　As far as any routine for me, it's always changing! There's just so much going on I can hardly keep up with my life! I've now color-coded my planner because if I didn't, I'd never keep up. I have to give myself an hour-by-hour schedule of things I have to do the night before for the next day. It's pretty fancy—I type it on the computer and everything. Then I follow it exactly, to the minute, so I can keep track of everything. I don't print it out—I keep track in the computer. I must stay superorganized!

Emma

Only 25 days and I get *MY LICENSE*! I'm so excited I can't wait. The only thing is that I'm secretly afraid I'll fail the test. Every single one of my friends so far has passed, and they say it's so easy, so I guess I should stop worrying. But the fact that they say that makes it worse. What if I do fail? My dad and I actually have to leave to go practice parallel parking soon. It's hard when the streets are all icy and snowy.

When I do get my license, my mom is going to give me her car. That's okay I guess. Of course, there's nothing really wrong with the car, but it's just not a brand-new sporty car like everyone else has. I mean, Sherelle always talks about her new Toyota, but that's so small. It's better for me really because I will save so much money on paying for a car and on insurance. All my friends are like broke from paying for their cars and that really stinks. And I have absolutely no money right now.

The thing about driving is that it will just be so cool to be able to go where I want when I want. I won't have to walk home in the freezing snow or rain or cold anymore. Like I'll be able to come and go as I please. At first I'm sure Mom will want me coming home at a reasonable time, but eventually she'll let me go be at the mall. And I can drive to school, which is a big deal. It will make school worth going to.

Kevin

Yesterday was a good example of why I hate school so much. It snowed pretty bad here and they did not let us out of school at all. It was sooooo ghetto! And then it took me like 30 min to get home instead of the usual 5 to 10 min. Actually it was so bad I couldn't even go anywhere tonight like out or anything. I would've hung out w/Cristina too since I feel like I wanna spend all my time w/her lately. So I was pissed but then me & Jake and my bro watched Jim Carrey in *Liar, Liar* and laughed our asses off so it turned out okay. Meanwhile today not much has been going on except I went w/my jerk bro, Neil, to the pet store to get some mice so he could feed his snake. Yeah, he has a stupid constrictor and it's pretty damn hungry too—he's a big-ass mouse eater. I can't watch when he feeds though b/c it is just way too nasty. Okay then later on we went over to Lazlo's place & played some cards for like an hour or two. Sometimes I think I could be like the biggest gambler in the whole freakin world b/c it is such a rush for me playing. Too bad tho Jake was the one who lost like 35 bucks—I'm only out like 25 cents or whatever. Ta ta

23

Teresa

Dear Diary,

Oh my God! It's happening! Today me and my dad went to Lawrence's game! As soon as we got there, right before the game started, we went to a pay phone inside the place so my dad could call my brother (he beeped him). Anyway, I was just standing there next to the phone booth area and all of a sudden this door nearby opened and out walked the *entire* Reds hockey team, with who right at the front? Lawrence! I hope he saw me!! I was *really* staring too. The Reds ended up losing 6–2 but it was Lawrence who scored both goals, which I think is sooooo awesome. I was cheering for him 100%.

Tonite I went over to Betsy Welsh's house. She's another field hockey player on my team and she was having this Winter Wonderland Sweet 16. I saw a lot of people there from the team like Sherelle and from other places. Actually, Betsy got the exact same DJ I had at my Sweet 16 in October. It was cool seeing all of the dancers again. She has soooo many cute guy friends actually, I was noticing . . .

Here's the funny part—I ended up hooking up w/this guy Damien, who is actually Sherelle's ex-boyfriend's second cousin or something like that. Everyone knows everyone and we just found ourselves together at the party at some point. I'm not quite sure how/why it happened—but it was fun!

Seeing Lawrence *and* hooking up w/Damien in one day—I can't handle it! Ha ha ha!

Katie

January 9
@ 10 P.M.

What a day! I've been up since 6:30 in the morning. My mom and I went to the salon together for a day of beauty. It was so relaxing. We spent a few hours there and I had my hair highlighted and got my eyebrows waxed. Then we went out to lunch and went shopping. Mom said she would get me a new suit since I have this new position in Community Club! Mom got a pair of shoes. It's such a good experience because we get a chance to bond a lot. My mom is like my friend as much as she is my mom. We have a very special relationship, I think.

Later on, Brad called around 5 o'clock to see if I wanted to go to the car wash with him and I said okay. I actually love the car wash and have since I was a little kid. So I told my dad we were leaving for 20 minutes or so but then we ended up driving around forever! The first 2 places we went were *closed* and then this 3rd place was self-service and it was like 20 degrees out. Forget that one! We blew it off & went to the mall instead, which was a good thing. I looked for a sweater at the Gap to replace this one I left in Florida by mistake. I didn't want my mom to find out that I lost it. Unfortunately, there were none left to replace it. Oh well. By now it was getting late, so I asked Brad to take me home.

Of course, that's when the torture started. My dad started in on me when I walked in the door. "Going to the car wash, huh? For an hour or more?" My little brother was teasing me too. "Did you steam up the windows, Katie?" I was soooo embarrassed. Lucky for me, my mom broke it up. I was mortified. Sometimes my family just doesn't know when to quit. Thank goodness for Mom!

Marybeth

January 10th

I have been thinking a lot the last couple of days. Since New Year's, I feel sort of disconnected from my parents a little. Especially Mom. I dunno what 4. Things are just different all of a sudden w/them like everything I'm learning or wanting as I get more freedom and responsibility is changing things. I mean, I know we don't *always* get along, but it bothers me more these days for some reason—I wonder Y? I found this poem that says what this feels like 2 me. . . .

I'm leaving now to slay the foe—
Fight the battles, high and low.
I'm leaving, Mother, hear me go!
Please wish me luck today.

I've grown my wings, I want to fly,
Seize my victories where they lie.
I'm going, Mom, but please don't cry—
Just let me find my way.

I want to see and touch and hear,
Though there are dangers, there are fears.
I'll smile my smile and dry my tears—
Please let me speak my say.

I'm off to find my world, my dreams,
Carve my niche, sew my seams,
Remember as I sail my streams—
I'll love you, all the way.

By Brooke Mueller

From Chicken Soup for the Teenage Soul

By the way—yesterday was a surreal moment at this Sweet 16 w/this girl Brittany, who goes to Joyce. It was surreal b/c her party was like this total mix of

friends and nonfriends. Me and Emma were there &
had a pretty funny time, laughing thru most of it.

Baxter

January 10
This weekend is so boring. Everyone has a party
to go to except me. I'm tired of always having to stay
home while everyone goes out. Not that being with
my mom and dad is bad, because I always laugh a lot
with them. They're great.

Megan called late last night. That was good, I
thought. And we talked for 45 minutes. But it really
wasn't good. All we talked about was school. Again.

I feel like watching TV, I guess. Sometimes I think
that maybe I watch too much, but then I don't care.
My mom doesn't say anything to me as long as I do
okay in school. Right now, my doggie Coconut is up
on my bed and she looks cute. I guess it's okay to be
alone even if I am bored. I'll see what's on.

Maybe I'll try calling Emma later.

p.s. By the way, this week is when I get into the
Honor Society. This is very cool. They're having this
induction ceremony and everything. I am still pretty
proud of what I have done. I think Megan will be im-
pressed when she hears I was up there.

Emma

Because of the snow, my mom wouldn't let me or my sister go out all day without her. She couldn't take us anywhere until late in the afternoon (we had a Sweet 16 to go to) and then she said that we should tell our friends to come over to our house instead. But that didn't matter. I don't think anyone really did much of anything today anyway. I was supposed to go to a girls' basketball game, but even that got canceled because of the snow. Everyone is just so pissed that it snowed, including me.

Yesterday the snow sucked the most. Because none of us were allowed to go out, Sherelle ended up hanging out with Bobby and that was it. Marybeth just stayed home and made cookies with M&M's in them. And then I couldn't even *talk* to Cliff because he was at work until really late.

Finally my mom agreed to drive me so Marybeth and I went over to this girl Brittany's house for her Sweet 16. She goes to Joyce HS, actually, but we know her through church and community stuff. Anyway, it was weird because Marybeth and I knew like *no one* at this party except Brittany and this one other girl, her name is Gwen Hirsh. We're at school w/her but we never ever talk. The only time we really hung out with Gwen was over the summer once because she was at Katie's parents' house by the

29

beach. Gwen goes to JFK and is *really* good friends w/Katie. But me and Marybeth don't like her at all. She's kind of snobby.

Ok here's what happened—last summer once she dissed Sherelle because of what she was wearing down by the beach! I don't think Gwen knew we heard her talking, but she called Sherelle trashy because of these pants Sherelle was wearing. Give me a break! Gwen didn't even know Sherelle that well. How could she say that? What a bitchy thing to do. Anyway, since that day we decided we hated her. Katie knows it too but whatever.

So the thing is, there we were at this Sweet 16, me and Marybeth, and it was Gwen who looked sooooo bad this time! She had on this like mini, mini brown skirt and tight top and she was dancing like a real hoochie and just looked all stupid. It was pretty hard not to laugh. Marybeth and I were laughing hard, and I think Gwen maybe knew because she ignored us completely. I mean, she couldn't even say "hi" so screw her. Marybeth agrees with me on this one. We're just making sure that she knows we hate her. I can't wait to see her at JFK after this. I just wish Sherelle could've seen it! She was at some field hockey Sweet 16.

Sometimes I think it bugs Katie that we treat Gwen this way, seeing as how they're such good friends and all that, but I can't care about that. I don't have to deal with Gwen if I don't want to. Not after she was the one who trashed one of my friends to begin with. Oh well. Whatever.

Billy

1-10

This weekend is turning out okay cause it turns out Ben & Deke called me after all and we all went drinking. We got hammered. It was awesome. I have so much fun with those guys. We can be completely out of our minds and out of control! Well, not out of control literally because we are obviously careful about not drinking and driving. I mean, at 17 I am certainly mature enough to handle myself. I think that this is the main thing that makes me different than some of the other kids in my class. I know how to do almost everything and I am willing to try everything. Like, I can study real hard, I can do good at sports, and I can also go out and have a really good time for myself while being responsible. I think a lot of kids fuck up a lot.

This week there are more rehearsals for the musical. I have this part in the chorus but that's cool. I didn't want anything major, just something so I could sing a little bit. I decided that I really like singing. It makes me feel good inside. I don't know why but it does. My mom and dad think it's a good thing that I keep it up too so I have something to show colleges other than just football. I guess that's because I'm not as good as Lee was so they don't know how I'll do getting in or something like that. I just know they want me to keep doing more and more stuff. Sometimes I think that's why I party too, so I can just be myself and let go of all this parent bullshit. I don't have to work hard or try to please anyone. It's just about me and me alone. I mean, I love my parents, but sometimes it just gets to me.

I can't be everything to everyone as much as I wish that I could be that way. I wish that all the time. But all that happens is I just find out how much *more* stuff there is that I need to do and learn. Like now. I have homework to do before it gets too late.

Jake

January 10

My dad was talking about his birthday today. It's not for a few weeks, but he was thinking about it anyhow. He's turning 47. I look at him and he seems so much older. It makes me feel sad all over. I wish he would get well.

This weekend went by too fast. Friday night was boring and all I did was have another snowball fight with my brother and sister. But it was good to see my uncle Charlie, who I haven't really seen since my cousin's funeral. Mom made dinner and he came over.

He seems a little less sad about Frankie than he did last week. Wow, has a lot been going on. I don't know why it seems like so much bad stuff is going on.

Yesterday afternoon I went over to Kevin's house and we had a Nerf gun fight in his basement. Then he and I went over to Lazlo's with Jonny. We played cards and shot pool. There were supposed to be a bunch of girls coming over to play around at Lazlo's house too, but no one showed up. And that is so stupid because these girls in our grade are always saying it's *our* fault for never hanging out. So fuck them. They blew it off not us. Oh well I have to go.

Kevin

1/11

I found out what happened to Cristina and all the girls from school on Sat. They were supposed to come hang w/me & Jonny & Lazlo & Jake but no they went out to drink and all a whole bunch of them oh well. I'm feelin so disoriented by everything going on lately. But um oh I was so pissed cause when I was talking to Cristina I realized I won't be able to see her for like a week b/c she's goin skiing this coming wkend and then on Monday we have off from school for Martin Luther King day. So I start bitching to her b/c I really wanna spend some time hanging out. Okay like this is how it is between me & her now. Like how we are w/each other. She was kiddin around and she starts talking to me about where she was hanging out on Saturday has a girl to guy ratio of like 1 to 9 and she says her chances of hooking up are so much better. And I couldn't believe she would say that to me while I'm like standing there showing her I'm mad. Then all of a sudden Cristina is like come on Kevin, you know I'm j/k, come on. And there I was all upset I had to laugh and she said come on again you know I love you. And our other friends Pam & Deb were standing there too and they heard the whole convo and they were like dying laughing at us both. So whatever I'm over it. Ta ta

Katie

January 12
@ 8:30 P.M.

Why is this week going by so slowly and it's only Tuesday? My workload is *HELL*. We've also been having rehearsals back-to-back for the last 2 days. I've decided that I don't like the director very much. I think this play should be a fun learning experience and the drama teacher/director Mr. Remmers is all business. We have 8 weeks to get the production on. Isn't that enough time to learn everything *and* have fun at the same time? And by the way, it's pretty interesting seeing Rachel Ross, my mortal enemy, every day. I am going to have to figure out some way to be nice to her at least while we're both doing *The Boy Friend*.

School is still tough. Starting this new year hasn't been a real smooth transition for me for some reason. I'm still having a significant amount of trouble in chemistry but I'm trying not to let it affect me. I'm trying to remind myself that one less than perfect grade is not going to kill me and that my life is more than what is down on a piece of paper.

Marybeth

January 12th

Well, life is picking up 4 me. I got a job @ Shopwell, this store in town. I start next Saturday and I am working noon to like 5, Sunday 11–5, and then on Monday nites after that 2 b/c I need the cash bad! The only thing about it that sux is that next Sun. I was supposed to drive my bro Mitch to school and now I can't.

Yesterday I reffed basketball and had a basketball game today. We got killed today, again. Ohhhh! Last nite I almost forgot who called me! TJ! We talked from 11–1:15. It was great! He was like well it only took me a million years to get ur # (from Emma). I was like saying I never thought he was serious about it and he was like of course I was. He is *HOTTTT*!

Teresa

Dear Diary,

Okay so a long time ago I went out w/my pal Gina's cousin Rusty, only we pretty much cooled off. We're friends now, although I haven't heard from him in a while. Well, tonite he beeped me! I couldn't believe it! He got home for his school winter break. Of course, it was kinda awkward since we haven't spoken really since we had that huge fight last August. But it felt really cool to connect and to be mature like we've moved on. I actually realized tonite that I miss him. Not as a boyfriend, but just miss him as a friend.

Rusty was the kind of guy who would cry w/me and be there for me through it all no matter what. I really respect what we had together. Somehow I hope we can get some of that back again. As a matter of fact, I still have a ticket stub from our very first date stuck up on my dresser mirror. We went to see this local band called Into Red Giant. We had a really good time only the truth is my attention wasn't really on the concert as much as it was focused on him. One look at my eyes would have given that one away!

It's too bad that I can't talk to Gina about any of these feelings. I just can't discuss him w/her—she gets all weird and awkward when I talk about Rusty and me. Oh well, it's probably just some twisted form of jealousy. She'll get over it.

Jealousy Jealousy

Emma:

Cliff's ex-gf makes me sooo jealous a lot of the time. Like if Cliff or any guy I have ever been with still talks to his ex-girl I HATE THAT! I resent these girls because they used to know Cliff like a long time ago and I haven't been around as long. You never know what might happen.

Kevin:

I get jealous when I see strangers hugging and kissing and shit b/c I really and truly hate how some people look perfect and I'm stuck here w/what I got.

Teresa:

I wish I wasn't as jealous as I am of people. I realize it's not right to envy others, but I just can't help it. Every time I see another person talking to someone I know and I like I get very very VERY jealous and I know this is crazy! I am jealous of people w/boyfriends, people skinnier than

me, people talking to my friends,
people w/better grades, and
everything else and I just can't
change that.

Jake:

I hate it when your girl talks to
other guys that like her. There was this
one time when Claudia did that right in
front of me. I was burning up inside.

Marybeth:

It's not like I ever get really jealous,
but it sux if I'm going out w/a guy + he's
like oooh look at that girl.

Billy:

I don't get jealous of people because I'm
cool w/my life. But I know if I were totally into
some hot girl I would get mad if someone moved
in on her before I got a chance.

Jealousy Jealousy

Katie:

Sometimes I feel jealous of Rachel Ross, like when she gets all the attention at the auditions for The Boy Friend or when they write up articles on her in the school paper. But I have to rise above my feelings and be a bigger and better person than her. That's all there is to it.

Baxter:

Other people seem to get everything their way, like girls and grades. Even though I'm trying hard, I can't always get those things and that makes me jealous of those people.

Jake

It's a new year and my life still sucks and there are still no women.

Yesterday I went to life-guarding class with Kevin and we did back boarding. Then I came home, did chemistry homework, watched HBO, and fell asleep. I have been so tired lately because I go to bed so late.

Today I woke up, went to school, came home, ate, went to work, got 2 leads, hit on this girl from work, got rejected, and came home.

Now I have more homework.

Emma

1/12, 8:08 p.m.

I am so pissed off at Baxter. I'm sitting here in my room just chilling and there's this paper I have to do and I have all this history homework. And I don't understand the directions for history so I thought maybe Baxter could help. But when I called, his brother Jerry answered and said, "Can he call you back?" And I was like, "Okay, whatever." And so then 5 minutes later he still hadn't called. So I called him again and then he was like, "What do you want?" THEN I was superpissed. He hadn't even done the homework yet or looked at the directions.

40

I hate it when someone is in such a rush to get off the phone with you. I just think that is like the rudest thing. All he had to say was, "I'll call you when I look at it." Then I wouldn't have been pissed. But he didn't do that. Instead he was just like, "I haven't done it. Bye." I seriously wanted to kill him for that.

The next time he calls me I am slamming the phone down in his ear. Or I'll just say, "I'll call you back later, Bax, okay?" And then I won't call back.

Okay maybe I am just making this big deal out of nothing and Baxter is just busy. Like if I were to mention this to him, he would probably laugh at me and tell me I was just being stupid. Things like that don't bother him for some reason. But they bother me. Oh well. Whatever. I have to get up early tomorrow and go to a meeting for student council.

p.s. As far as things with me and Sherelle, they are getting better these days. They have since the new year started. She beeps and calls me and I call her now too. I'm glad because I don't want to keep fighting or for her to think I'm mad at her or something. She wrote me this cool letter today in class and told me this kid Gregory wants me. She makes me laugh! I don't even know Greg and I love Cliff anyway!!!

p.p.s. I think I'm going to call Baxter back again. I'm still pissed.

Baxter

Today was busier than usual. I had to stay after school until after 7:30 for yearbook. We were sorting out candid photos that different kids had submitted. Sometimes that can be a lot of fun, but I was tired.

Then I got home and the phone rang. It was Emma and she was doing the history homework and wanted help. I hadn't even started it! She made me freak out because I realized I was way behind. When I was on the phone with her, I looked over the assignment for the first time. He assigned us like 5 chapters. Even now, I only have gotten through half of it. I'm probably screwed. We'll probably have a pop quiz or something and I will be dooooooooomed. This never happens to me. Well, it happens lately. Physics sucks. I got a D and a C+ on two different quizzes. It's so hard. What's up with that?

The weatherman says it's supposed to snow more this week. I am crossing my fingers. I would be so happy to have more snow days and less school. I'm sick of being stressed out about grades. It would be nice to stop for a few days.

Billy

The work isn't hard lately, but since the winter break homework just seems to be coming in larger quantities. For ex. this week I was assigned like 3 papers in 3 dif. classes. And okay, it's easy, but it's such a pain in the ass. I mean, nothing is that HARD for me b/c I basically understand most of what's going on. It's just the actual doing of the work. That's my problem. And once lacrosse starts in the spring—oh boy—I will be way worse off than I am now, with no time left. In order to remedy that, I need to work harder to attain a straight-A average so I have a shot at a good college.

Of course, Miss Gifford will prob. be the one to fuck things up for me. She hasn't gotten any better since the year has gone on. Not at all. Last fall, I dreaded her English class and I still dread her class. Teresa says I don't give her a chance. For whatever reason, Teresa loves Miss Gifford, But I still hate her. Okay, maybe to hate someone is a little too strong. To be absolutely honest, I don't really think I *hate* anyone. I guess to hate Miss Gifford b/c she assigns a lot of work I don't wanna do is just immature on my part. Still, it can really piss me off, right?

I'd better get to work.

Teresa

Dear Diary,

I was talking to Miss Gifford after class today and we were deciding that I have an absolute obsession for the arts. She is soooooo nice. I really feel like she just understands me. Today in class we were discussing Hemingway and *A Farewell to Arms* (the book we are reading right now) and I realized that I really like his style of writing. I like being able to say a lot with just a few words, like he does. I think that's why I like writing poetry too. I can use it to convey ideas and feelings.

Sometimes I think that the reason I write is so that I can be better emotionally. I used to feel so empty inside last year, like everyone was against me. Now I feel like I can say what's on my mind. And it totally helps to have a teacher you can confide in too. She reads a lot of my poems, even the ones that weren't for assignments. She is nice about that. Sometimes when I'm not sure about who I am writing to or why I am writing, she helps me figure it out, and she was also the first person who really encouraged me to read other people's poems, like Emily Dickinson or Maya Angelou. I need help figuring it out! Whether it's about friendship, dreams, goals, insecurity, depression, I like knowing what's going on in other people's minds. It's great. Now, if only I could figure out what's going on in someone like Lawrence Gillooly's mind! Then I'd be *REALLY* great!

Here's a poem I typed last nite. It's okay I guess—it's different for me. Miss Gifford said I should try one w/out rhyming for a change. I could sometimes and not other times. But it felt really freeing to try it. I'm not really sure who it's about. Maybe Kevin, who I don't like in that romantic way anymore but who will always seem so perfect to me in all ways, maybe him.

DONE

Did I hear him speak from a distance?
Did I see him?
There was no face, no eye.
No mouth, no sense.
Music plays all around me
And inside me, running like water.
He is invisible but I can feel him.
Won't the sunlight show me where he is?
Will the music play a path to him?
I want my eyes to fill up with him,
Just like my heart.
Let the sun shine now.
Give me a head start.
But the sky is darkening.
The clouds are gathering.
The music has stopped.
All that I can see and hear
Is the cold rustle of a tree,
And it is mocking me.
Where are you, my love?

How can you leave me so?
All alone and desperate, with no place to go?
Waiting, I breathe into the silence.
And the music finally does begin again,
But it is different now.
In it, I don't hear your voice.
You left me alone, without a choice.
I must play on by myself.
And beyond music and the sun
That rises just for me now,
Everything stays the same,
Except our love
That is done.

Kevin

1/13

I've been like really melancholy lately and easily pissed off too like I will tend to either look into stuff thinking about it for a really long time or else I will just be moody. I guess maybe it has to do w/the fact that it's winter and all that stress and I know a lot of people would agree w/me on this.

So anyway, today I come home from school and swim practice and I walk in the door to see my dad there w/Zoe, kind of dozing off while she did homework. So I thought I could talk to him right there about what's pissing me off in school, w/friends, w/girls cause it didn't seem like he was doing much of anything else & I started talking. And he was listening for a while and I was going into it and then Zoe interrupted me and he stops me & says why don't I just finish my story later. So I was like, okay no biggie, I can go off and just keep thinking about things and get back to it another time that nite. But then I went into the kitchen and I saw that there was like no dinner there for me. I asked where was the food, and my dad said he didn't know and my mom was like nowhere around. So once again I pull this freezing spaghetti sauce and shit out of the fridge and put it together to make like this nasty reheated stored dinner. This is like every nite I am eating alone we never have dinner together and no one ever leaves stuff out for me. It's like I'm getting the cold shoulder or something and like Zoe, Neil, and everyone else are the ones who get attention paid to them.

I know I sound jealous, and maybe I am, but I really think I am seriously lacking the attention that everyone else around here gets. I mean, you could give my parents a survey about who I am and what I am interested in and I swear they would not have a single clue what the fuck is up w/me—they would fail in a heartbeat. I truly feel alone in my house. I am trying so hard all the time to do the right thing, I swear, and meanwhile like my brother Neil all he can do is be an asshole and break shit and cause trouble. That's just not fair. I'm sitting here w/a higher GPA than any of my brothers or sisters, *and* a job, *and* mad schoolwork, which they NEVER tried to do, *and* swimming, which I am totally excelling in, *and* helping my dad around the house, which they NEVER do. What's left for me to do differently before my parents notice it? It's just really frustrating b/c I am like in tears now just writing this.

I try to understand why would they leave me on my own so much and I guess they just figure other of the kids like Zoe b/c she's younger need more attention than me and I am pretty independent and don't need as much attention. But I do!!! A human that has no human compassion at times from his own family and not just from friends, even if they're pretty cool, will only perish. Thank God for Jake, right, but I need attention from other people too.

I guess it is true that only the strongest survive and that I probably just have to suck this up like everything else and just make my life the best I can make it with or without anyone else's help. I wouldn't mind help once in a while though or maybe just a "good job" from Mom or Dad. They always have these excuses about not having enough time and that they are too busy.

I just wanna know why some things are how they are and why I always end up feeling alone and no matter how much it hurts, or how much or long I might cry, or what others might think I have to survive this shit and never let it bother me to the point of my descent or anything. Okay I have no choice in the matter, I have to go up and only up and that's what I want and that's what I am keeping on striving to achieve yes the best of me and of what I possess. Ta ta

Jake

My brother Nate used up all the hot water in the shower this morning and I woke up late and got NOTHING. I was pissed and disappointed.

Went to school as usual but of course any woman I am interested in would rather be with other guys like older guys. I went to work today and hit on that girl again. She felt bad. Got 3 leads. Came home and played N64 007 and drank hot chocolate that was excellent. I am so glad because I will be getting a nice paycheck tomorrow.

Today on the way to work, Mom and I were talking more about my dad. For the last 10 months he has been in this special study with medicines at the hospital. He doesn't know if he is taking this real medicine or not. They're testing it out. It won't be until the summer that he knows for sure if he can take the real stuff. Right now it's gotten a little worse too—he can't even really hold himself up with his arms, so I see that he gets weaker every day. I just try not to think about it so much.

For now I am just sitting here, looking out the window and praying for snow.

I hope snow comes so we miss school tomorrow.

Katie

I haven't skipped a day of school from going home sick in 13 years and now I am home sick with cramps! This is *NOT* fun at all. I went down to the bathroom 2nd period and got these cramps that made me cry from my period. So then I went to the nurse and she sent me home after gawking with a bunch of teachers about how pale and clammy I looked— thank you very much! The nurse's office is next to the teacher lounge and so everyone was staring at me!!! I told the nurse there was no way I could go home because I had this big chemistry lab that I *absolutely* could not miss, but she just told me to be quiet. Mom picked me up. I hurt so bad, I took Motrin and drank this tea and slept for 4 hours.

Later on I felt much better of course and went to the National Honor Society induction ceremony. It was nice. They had it at this banquet hall with a real nice dinner. Mom was so proud of me and at least four different teachers came up to her and said wonderful things about me. Paul and Patti made me cards. Dad was away on a business trip, but he changed his flight home and made it back in time to catch the end of the ceremony. Brad gave me roses, of course. Big surprise!

Baxter

January 13

I just got back from the Honor Society induction. It was fun. It was held in this big hotel so everyone wore suits and nice outfits. Today in school Megan came up to me again and said she was psyched for me. That made me feel really good inside.

At the ceremony everyone stood on this stage and they read off our names and gave us certificates. Katie and Teresa were both there too. Dinner was ok. It was some kind of stuffed chicken. The only bad part of the night was driving home. My mom lost control of the car because the roads are so icy. It's pretty bad outside. I'm praying for no school tomorrow.

Teresa

Jan 14

Dear Diary,

We have off today because it's snowing outside! Last nite I attended the Honor Society inductions. I went over there w/my friend/neighbor Stephanie. Well, she's my ex-friend these days because of her spending every minute w/her boyfriend but we went together anyhow.

I'm really happy to be off today. I'm feeling sick and need this day to catch up on homework, my

51

health, sleep, etc. I think I *may* be getting the flu. Mom thinks we'll probably be off from school tomorrow too. It's snowing pretty hard out there. But either way, I won't go if I feel this crappy.

Marybeth

January 14th

We don't have school today b/c of the snow and I guess that's pretty cool 4 me! The story of my life right now is that I've talked to TJ *every night* this week so far since the weekend. It is so great. I went to watch him and the guys' basketball team last nite. He got like 5 rebounds and looked so *HOT* out there on the court. I was so happy for him. The guys' team is like soooo much better than our team—we're pretty bad these days. Anyway, I hope hope hope he calls again 2-nite.

I am actually praying that we *DO* have school tomorrow. I can't stand just sitting around at home being so bored w/nothing 2 do. I would rather at least be near TJ so we could talk and I could check him out!!! I wanna play my game w/him.

I guess the only weird thing going on these days is that kid Rick Wright is still on my case. He sent me another e-mail today, which made me mad. But really he says he's the one who's mad b/c we "used to talk" and now all we do is like pass each other in the hall w/out saying n e thing. He wants it to go back to the way it used to be and that we could be talking again. Doesn't he get it? He always ends up apologizing but the truth is that he's the one who gets all pissy anytime I am busy like I don't make time for him on purpose or something. I can't start talking to him a lot because all that happens is that even if we're just hanging out like not physical or n e thing, it ends up meaning more 2 him than it does 2 me and we've been thru all that already!

Ok so maybe I'm just a "heartless bitch" (his words for me, which makes me laugh still!) but I can't deal w/this crap anymore. And I want to spend my time now w/this guy TJ who seems nicer and more my kind of guy.

Jake

January 14
NO school today! I loved it. I did NOTHING. I slept in late. Then I got dressed in my sweats and jeans and went outside to play in the snow. I went outside and started throwing snowballs at my neighbor. We wrestled in a snowbank and got all wet. Then I came inside to warm up. My dad said he was watching me from his bedroom window.

Some friends of my older brother Nate came by and they had some dirt bikes, so I went with them and we did wheelies in the snow. I had more fun with them than I do with my own friends these days. Afterward, I came home and decided to skip work though. It was too messy outside. I'm feeling tired. Maybe we'll have off tomorrow!

Katie

January 14
@ 11 P.M.

SNOW DAY!!! This is awesome. I have done *nothing* all day long. Brad called a minute ago to see if I wanted to go to the movies, but I can't. It's a school night. I don't feel like going out anyway. I don't even feel like writing right now—so I won't.

Kevin

1/14

Today kicks ass b/c we have no school at all and I am soo freakin happy. The only bad part is that it is soo dangerous outside that I can't really go anywhere in my car or anything. I just sorta slept late and played around the house chilling all day.

I've been thinking more about things w/Cristina these days and I keep changin my mind back & forth like sometimes I think it would be so cool to be w/her and other times I know it's better if we just stay friends cuz that's so cool. I would do anything to go out w/her if I knew that everything about our relationship would stay the same if the romance didn't work out, but that's impossible of course. Everything changes once you go down that road but I would still try if Cristina was willing to try w/me. Ta ta

Billy

Snow everywhere and we are out of school, which is excellent. My dad of course will not let me drive anywhere though and he doesn't want to drive either because it is so icy, *SO* I am stuck here. I called Baxter to see what he was doing and he said he was just hanging out playing N64. Deke called me up to see if I wanted to go play touch football in the snow, but I blew it off. I called Lee my brother at college and he doesn't have much snow where he is. I guess I should do some homework since I am way behind in chemistry and need to read like the whole book *Farewell to Arms*, which I hate. Sometimes snow days are so good because you can play around, but then I feel guilty like maybe there's something more important I should be doing. Times like this I *really* wish I had a gf so we could get close and keep warm.

Baxter

January 15

Another *SNOW DAY!* That means we will end up having a 5-day weekend because Monday is Martin Luther King Day.

There's a foot of snow outside. It's beautiful but no one could go outside last night because of the weather. It's very icy. All I'm doing is just sitting here with my N64—chilling out. Funny!

Maybe I should call and see what Megan is doing today.

Emma

1/15, 12:00 p.m.

Today we had off from school again and Cliff took me to the movies. We went to see this movie *Varsity Blues* with that guy who plays Dawson on *Dawson's Creek*. It opened today actually so we weren't sure we'd be able to get a ticket but we did. Plus it was rated R so we didn't know if they'd let us in but they did. It seems pretty stupid to make an R-rated movie that is mainly for kids my age, who are under the age limit. I thought the movie would be better than it was too. They made such a big deal out of it.

When I walked outside the movie theater to wait for my dad, who was picking me back up, I saw the old girlfriend of my old boyfriend Chuck from 8th grade. She is so gross and I hate her so much and she hates me too. She's ugly too. When she saw me standing there outside the movies she gave me the *NASTIEST* look ever. I thought it was a pretty funny thing to do considering I was standing there with Cliff, my boyfriend now. I am so sure she will call Chuck up like right away and tell him that she saw me with this other guy. She is such a gossip too. But of course why should I care because I don't need Chuck or anything to do with Chuck anymore *especially* not her!

I am so glad to be out of school right now but I kind of wish we had it so I wouldn't have to babysit my little brother. Even if we had a delayed opening that would be good too. That means like school starts a lot later, like at 10 or so, and classes all are shorter. Yesterday babysitting was all I did and now I have to go home and do it again so my parents can go somewhere. I hate watching Ronnie sometimes—he is such a pain. He always wants you to play with him and then he can never play all by himself. And I get bored easily on snow days. There really is so little to do, and no one can go out in the icy streets and everyone's parents are at work. When I was talking to Marybeth on the phone yesterday, we were like ready to scream we were so bored. I told her she should come over to my house but she couldn't. We talked for like a few hours though, and online too once or twice. I can't believe we don't have school for like 4 days now. Monday is a holiday. I still have to go to my hockey game and manage on Monday though.

So Cliff told me today that he's getting a new schedule for work. I am hoping that maybe this means he will take off Sundays so we can hang out at least one of the weekend days but I don't know. I don't know what he's planning for this weekend—I think he'll go drinking with his friends and I will hang out with mine. But that's ok to be separate because we just spent time together already. I'll deal with it.

Emma + Cliff

Jake

January 15

Yeah baby! Off again. I'm loving this. 5-day weekend for us! We have off now Thursday, Friday, Saturday, Sunday, AND Monday. So cool. Martin Luther King Day. How I love that man. He has a dream and now we have off from school.

Today I did nothing. Again. But tonight I went to

see *Varsity Blues* with Kevin and some other friends. That movie really kicked ass. Our friend May, the one who has the pool table in her house, has one of her cousins in town named Bethany and we all went together.

I really wanted to hook up w/Bethany because she was really good-looking and fun to be with. But when we all sat in the movie theater, my other friend Cristina spent the whole time hitting me. Cristina kept on punching me—it was so dumb. I wished she was punching Kevin instead. I mean, they're the ones who are supposed to be together now. There was no way I could hook up with anyone because of stupid Cristina. I couldn't even try—it was so pitiful. And now Bethany is leaving tomorrow. I am thinking about asking her to the semiformal though. She only lives a few towns away. Maybe she'll come back soon and we can get together at a party or something.

Good Parties vs. Bad Parties

Kevin:

Good pARty time is when you get All shithoused & spend hours clubbin w/some cute girl or listening to house music or mAybe it's just when you hAve lAughs w/some good friends it depends, but A bAd pARty is def. like when there is <u>nothing</u> going on And people ARe stAnding ARound w/nothing to sAy & thAt is the worst Absolutely no doubt.

Emma:

The best kind of parties are drinking parties but I can't really go to drinking parties because I am too afraid I will get caught, so whatever. A bad party is always when you see like one of your ex-boyfriends standing there with another girl and she is so butt ugly that you just want to die. Also a bad party is when you end up being the 3rd wheel like I was w/marybeth and Snerelle, but things are different now so that isn't an issue.

Good Parties vs. Bad Parties

Baxter:

A party is a party! I like a party no matter what!

Katie:

I like surprise parties best of all! And I'm not into drinking, so I think that just talking and hanging out is the most fun. I've been going to so many Sweet 16 parties this year! A bad party is when everyone is so drunk that they start doing stupid things to each other like talking too loud or getting into fights for no reason. I hate it when Brad drinks at parties.

Marybeth:

Drinks + guys + laughs + friends = fun, fun, fun!

Billy:

When I am with guys from the team we get together and go wild—there is so much action it's a great time until the girls and the beer disappear. We don't calm down until 4 or 5 a.m. Total craziness! And I won't hang for even 5

Good Parties vs. Bad Parties

minutes if I think a party might be bad, which is usually when there are no ladies. If that's so, I gotta go.

<u>Teresa</u>:

I like to be surrounded by <u>lots</u> of my friends and that usually makes a party good for me. Actually, getting <u>ready</u> for the party is a big part of it too. I like fixing my hair, finding the right outfit, getting my nails done, and all that. I wanna look good b/c you never know who you could meet! It could be sooooo good—you never know! Only when you don't hook up w/someone or see some cute guy, that's when a party isn't so good. But even then it can still turn out ok. My gfs like Wendy & Gina always know how to cheer me up when I don't meet someone—which is all the time!!!

Good Parties vs. Bad Parties

Jake:

Good party: Vodka or some other drinks, hot women, house music

Bad party: Seeing Claudia with another guy, no dancing, stupid assholes acting stupid

Marybeth

Tae bo info # 1-800-72 —

It's so late right now. It's already 2:30 A.M. and I am so awake still. This is not cool at all. I am watching infomercials on TV. There's this guy Billy something & he has this video workout tape I think I might get. I dunno. I feel fat. I need to get motivated. It's esp. not cool to be up this late when I have basketball practice tomorrow *early* even tho it's the wkend—I have to get up @ 9:30 A.M. + then start work at Shopwell too later on. I have so much going on all of a sudden.

Tonite I talked again to TJ. God do I want him. It's so cool tho b/c I never have to call him, he always calls me. I don't even have his # so it's great! Later on Sherelle and Bobby came over & we went out for a while. We went to this hotel party, which is when someone rents a room and has alcohol and stuff there. But it was bad and the people were so random & we left and just came back here to hang out.

We had off school again today b/c of an official snow day even tho it didn't even snow. It sucked b/c it was supericy and then it got to be like 40° and then everything turned to slush. What a mess.

Katie

Another snow day and it's not even snowing? I can't believe this! I'll be out of school for 5 days by the time we go back. Wow. Today was a little busier than yesterday. I spent the whole day with Brad.

First, he picked me up around 10:30 and we went to the mall. I got a new purple sweater and we had lunch together and shopped for him. He wanted to get a sweater too! Then we went back to my house and hung out for a little while before going to the movies. Or at least we wanted to go to the movies. The thing about going to the movies with Brad is that he can NEVER decide what he wants to see and so we end up disagreeing all the time. When he has to see a movie he doesn't like he (a) sleeps or (b) gets really fidgety so we end up having to leave the theater. He finally agreed to see *Varsity Blues* and even liked it a little I think. He was well behaved. We were soooo lucky too because he left the lights on in his Jeep and we thought the battery would have been dead—but it was fine! Of course after a whole day together the very best part was still to come. I can't believe what happened next!

So Brad's best friend Tim is having his 17th birthday and so Brad wanted to do something really special. The thing is that Tim wanted to get a stripper very badly for some reason. He always wanted to go to this strip club called Foxes, and he talked about it all the time—it was nuts! So Brad got this idea of how to trick him.

First, he pulled a ski hat over Tim's head and put him into Brad's Jeep. And even though Tim didn't know it, the rest of us got together (me, Gwen Hirsh, and her bf who is also Brad & Tim's friend Ted, Tim's older sister Lacey, Brad & Tim's other friends Keith and Roger, and a few other friends). The guys pretended to be taking him to a stripper—like they'd ever get into one of those places anyhow! So when they had blindfolded Tim in the car they took him to the recreation center where Brad teaches and pretended like it was this other place. They had it all set up with really loud music playing and Tim had absolutely no idea what was happening! Then the best part happened because my friend Gwen started to dance around Tim like she was a stripper! He was literally thanking his friends because he really thought his wish was coming true. He wanted to know where was the beer!

Gwen was having an impossible time keeping in her laughter but she kept it in and started putting whipped cream on him. He was really getting into it! Meanwhile her boyfriend Ted, who is also friends w/Tim, was laughing too. Everyone was. So there we were and all of a sudden in the middle of everything, Brad pulls off Tim's blindfold so he now sees what's happening! It was hysterical. I know he was sooooo embarrassed for having believed he'd been taken to a strip club, especially Foxes. What a good surprise! His facial expression was unforgettable—we will never forget that! Of course, he was so horrified at the same time, but he cleaned up and kept partying. There wasn't really drinking. We were having a good time without all that. All in all, a fun night.

Teresa

Jan 16

Dear Diary,

I still don't feel well. We had no school Friday and now it's the weekend and *I HATE BEING SICK!* I was so psyched because Hammy called me today from U Colorado. He was wondering what I was up to—and he asked how I was feeling. Wasn't that sweet?

Unfortunately, there are still no guys in my life, even with Hammy calling me up. I think my feelings for him have changed anyway. I don't really have a crush on him anymore. I mean, he's 20 and that's like not a real possibility! And he lives in Colorado, which isn't exactly close by.

I mean, I do like Hammy as a person. He's just not this "out of reach" fantasy, that's all. Hammy's just more like a friend. Wow, I wish I could just find the *right* person, is that so much to ask? I think my mom wonders the same thing. Nothing has happened so far with that guy Lawrence from the Reds. And I miss Kevin a lot these days because we never see each other and that makes me sooo sad. Especially when we have sooo much in common! But he isn't interested at all, I know that now by heart.

Even though my love life is a little shaky, I did get *AWESOME* news today about working. My brother Vincent's ex-girlfriend Tara, the one who promised that she'd try to help me get a job at KidCare where she works, called. Finally! And *I GOT THE JOB!!!!* I didn't even have to really apply! After she called me, my new boss called me up and asked me to come in on Monday even though it's a holiday so she could meet me and talk with me. She also wants me to meet the kids at the center and get to know the rest of the staff a little bit and just get a feel for the place. I am so excited! And I'm going to be making ok money so it really works out. Actually, I think I'll just throw myself into my new job and maybe then I can forget about the whole situation with no men in my life! Oh well!

Billy

1-16

With all the snow it's given me all this time to think about how fast time is flying. I just think that there are so many more things I want to do. There is no time left to do them. I am so dreading my workload still. Having so much time off only makes it worse too. I know how busy I will be when I get back. My dad is putting all this pressure on me to work when I have free time too. I just don't know.

Baxter called me to see what was going on. He wanted me to go to the mall, but I didn't feel like going. All I ever end up doing is playing games in the arcade anyhow. I don't really need any new clothes or anything. My mom got me some stuff at Christmas so I don't. He says I never want to hang out anymore. Maybe he's right. He's still a good friend though. It's just that things are changing, like I said. Maybe we can hang out tomorrow. I'm just glad we have this 5-day weekend.

Shit, I can't believe I still haven't read *A Farewell to Arms*! I better read at least half of it before I go back to Miss Gifford's class or I will be in deep trouble.

Kevin

So after the Friday night episode w/Jake practically jumping on May's cousin ha ha, I was giving him such shit today on the phone it was sooo funny. He was pissed b/c he said Cristina was punching him or something so he had no chance but I don't remember that happening at all oh well. Pretty much since Fri. it's been downhill.

Ok since the other day I've been like steaming mad at my parents and my whole family really cuz I am just pissed about bein left out and all and so when I found out we were going to some party for my dad that just made me madder. It's a surprise party and even though his birthday is like 2 months away, my mom insisted on having it way, way early so he'd never guess about it. Ok so then we go late at nite tonite & there were like 180 total people there it was so out of control! I must admit that he was looking so so so so surprised when he walked in w/my mom and it was worth it and I stopped being pissed so it ended up cool. Yeah other than those things, the whole wkend so far has been boring and I'm way tired. Ta ta

Jake

After a great night's rest I woke up refreshed and ready for work. Today was the *BEST* day! I went in and got my paycheck at the mortgage company, so that made me superhappy, and then Mom took me out shopping at the mall, which is something she has not done in a long long time.

We shopped and ate lunch together. We've been talking more lately. My mom bought me a lot of clothes and she also let me drive, which was great. It was cool because even though the ground was slushy and wet, she trusted me in the car. That made me feel good.

I was supposed to go over to the Morans' to help them out w/Kevin's dad's surprise party today but Kevin told me to blow it off. He did it already. I went though and it turned out great. All these people showed up, like 200 people. The speeches that everyone's family and friends made were special too. I was thinking it might be nice to have a party or something like that when my dad's birthday happens in a few weeks but I don't know what my mom thinks.

Mr. Moran has done so much for me and my whole family. I don't know how we could ever repay him for all that he has done. So after the party, we came home. And then Katie came by, which was nice. I haven't really seen her much lately without a bunch of people around. Kevin was here too. We watched some movie on TV—I don't even know the name.

After we brought Katie home, me and Kevin decided to go get hot chocolate and a box of doughnuts and we just ate and drank. Kevin left at 12:30. After that I went online and got the biggest surprise of the whole night. I think it was an even bigger surprise than Mr. Moran's party. I had an e-mail from Rebecca Rinaldi—she is this really hot girl in my class. We are friends of course but I don't think of it much. She is very sweet.

Rebecca asked me to the prom. And of course I said yes because I want to go and she is cute. I think I want her now.

Katie

January 17
@ 4 P.M.

I think today we're going skiing. I hate skiing. I can't ski!

I figure though, if I can't ski, at least I can look good doing it, or not doing it, and so yesterday I went w/Mom to this outlet store, SnowTown, to get some new ski clothes. We spent a lot of $$$ but it was worth it! Now I look like a real ski bunny. When we were at the outlets, we also stopped by the pool store

72

and got Mr. Moran a birthday present for his party Saturday.

It was a great surprise party, by the way. I was so happy for Kevin and his whole family that it turned out so well—with soooo many people! Kevin's dad is such an important part of the community and he does so much to help people so it's nice to give something back to him. Sherelle and her boyfriend Bobby were there for a while, but they took off after only like an hour. I thought that was so rude, but Kevin didn't say anything. Actually, Kevin seemed kind of out of it all night, though I don't know why exactly. Even later on, when Kevin and Jake and I rented a movie, he was still acting distant. We didn't hang out for very long.

But enough about last night! Right now I am on the road to go ski with Brad and his friends. The mountain is only 3 hours away. I don't even remember which slopes he said we're going to! It's funny because I'm the one person in the car (Tim, Lacey, Gwen, and Ted came too) who knows where we're going even though I don't know where we're going! I'm just good at remembering directions and sometimes that annoys Brad because I don't even drive yet! But I still make a point of staying awake so I can help him. He needs me. If I fall asleep for even 5 minutes he'll start going 90 miles per hour and that makes me crazy! I have to pay attention or we might get lost.

Baxter

So far this weekend has been okay. I have spent a lot of time with my mom and dad. My brother Jerry decided not to come home even though he has a long weekend at school and he's pretty close by.

Yesterday I wanted to go out with Billy but he was busy. Today he was less busy and so we hung out together. It was fun! I was glad to see him. The only bad thing is that sometimes he jokes too much about my family. He's always saying that I'm too close to my parents and no one should be that close to their parents. He jokes about how I have to be home for dinner and says I'm weird just because I like to hang out at home and that I sleep with my dog Coconut. I don't think I am weird though. I don't know where they got this idea that my family is perfect. We're just normal, that's all. Emma says I should just ignore him so I will.

One major highlight of yesterday was going to shop for a little while at the mall—where I got BRIT-NEY'S NEW CD! It is so good. It even came with a poster. She is so HOT! I love her.

Emma

Right now I am so pissed off at my friend Roger I can't even think right. Ok so here's what happened, we talked about going to the semiformal together. It's coming up on February 19th and he said he would go with me. The reason I would go with Roger is because Cliff said he didn't want to go. Ok but now it's like 3 days after when I asked Roger and I heard now he's actually going with this other girl Heather. So I'm like whatever, I didn't know about her. But when I asked him about it, he just said he didn't care and he would go with me. And now I am like totally confused about who is going with who. But NOW he changed his mind, he does want to go with Heather, and so he has a date and I am stuck with no date for the semi. He hasn't actually asked her yet, but I know he will and all I can say is I really and truly hope she says NO. I would be so happy if that happened. Here he tried to screw me over and I would like to see that he is the one who ends up getting screwed.

Maybe I should ask this other guy Jacob who goes to this private school in our town. I've known him since like 4th grade—he's nice. Or maybe I'll ask my other friend Justin. Times like now I totally wish that Scott hadn't moved to Florida because it would be so awesome to go to the dance with him of all people.

Whatever. Even if I don't end up getting a date, I am still never talking to Roger again I swear. I mean, it would be a totally different situation if he hadn't promised me and if Cliff would be willing to go of course.

Apart from the semi thing, things with Cliff are going very, very well. I just talked to him earlier on the phone and he was telling me he loved me and all that, which is so cool of him. He knows it makes me feel good to hear that. We were talking about how great it is going to be when I get my license—in only 17 days! Then I can go see Cliff whenever I want. I will be the one who can drive us to the movies and stuff. Look out, February 3. That's all for now!

marybeth

January 17th

I have not been this PO'ed about n e thing in a really really long time! I mean like superpissed. So I was over at this girl Amy Flanagan's tonite. She's this new friend from The Mix & we hang out @ lunch a lot. On my way out tho, that guy Big Paulie called and that was good b/c he wanted me 2 hang out. So I called him back when I got over 2 Amy's place. I decided to go meet him instead of heading to the movies & we hung out & eventually we hooked ↑ and more "stuff."

I think he is a real dick because all he wanted was sex. I mean, he knew that I meant "no," but if I had said "yes" he totally would have. So then a little bit after, he dropped me off to go meet his friends & drive them somewhere. Okay, he said he'd be back again but he's not here. It's like ten minutes later and he's still gone. I think he's such an asshole for doing this 2 me. I thought he was all nice, but I guess not.

So today turned out bad 4 me. This sux & I really hope someone else calls me so I don't have to just sit here. I wanna go out more. Maybe Lance will call and we can hang out at the Silverado or something.

Earlier I had my 2nd day at Shopwell. The job is okay. I'm a cashier so they had me in training all day yesterday. It's tiring but I get ok $$. I need to make $$ to get a better car.

How I Feel About Money

Emma:

Um money is always a good thing to have and I always try to save all the money I get from babysitting because I hate asking my parents for it all the time. Also I don't look for guys with money. I had a bf once with a lot of money but he treated me like crap. I would rather him be poor and treat me right. I am not gonna want my husband to support me—I'm gonna want to be able to do it on my own.

Kevin:

I need soooo much money LOL, no reAlly I just wish I had like mAd cAsh All to myself thAt I got And I eArned or just won or something but cAsh thAt wAs mine And thAt I didn't get it from my pArents or Anything like thAt.

How I Feel About Money

Katie:

Honestly I don't worry about money at all. I should but I don't. I know I sound spoiled but my parents have given me the right values. I know how hard they worked for what they have. Someday I will do the same, which is work hard, support my family comfortably, and give my children what they need.

Baxter:

This year I realize more that money doesn't grow on trees. I want to pay for more of my own stuff. I have a nice supply that I hope will get bigger when I get a job next summer.

Teresa:

Who doesn't just love $$?? I do!!! I put every single one of my paychecks in the bank to save up for college stuff and a car. Plus, I still have bonds and CDs and stuff in my bank

How I Feel About Money

account that haven't matured yet
so things r looking ok
moneywise!!!

<u>Jake:</u>

Want it, love it, need it. I need to
work harder so I can help out at home,
like make extra money for my mom for
little things. I know money from
snowblowing or the mortgage company isn't
much, but Dad says he is proud of me
for working hard.

<u>Marybeth:</u>

The cash flow's been decent 4 me prob.
b/c I am working so much. I think it
gives me more independence so I don't
have to ask my 'rents for it. I like
buying stuff and if I wanna buy stuff I
have to put something into it meaning
work. When I want something that's
around $30 that means I have to work
for like 5 hours.

How I Feel About Money

<u>Billy:</u>

   Lots of $$$ = cool car, hot girls, and everything else I want. I mean I don't wanna seem shallow, but $$$ is the answer to so many things.

Teresa

Dear Diary,

I can't stop thinking about my job—I am sooooo excited to work w/kids! Maybe that's because school is sort of a slump right now. At least this weekend it feels that way. I talked to Gina's cousin Rusty again and that was cool. He's sort of back in the picture a little I guess. I don't know.

Today I spent the afternoon working on this essay for class. We're still finishing up the Hemingway novel, but we had an extra creative-writing assignment. We could write about anything. The teacher wanted us to write about something we felt strongly about—it could be anything. I didn't have any brilliant ideas. I wrote about how I am feeling these days.

ROLLER COASTER

When they first strap you into a seat on the roller coaster, everything's fine. Of course, your hands get a little sweaty from the anticipation and your forehead perspires because you are nervous. But you don't move. You stay perfectly still, waiting for the roller coaster to start, to edge up that first hill, all the way. . . .

Once it starts to inch and twist down the track, you feel the roller coaster inside you completely, tingling and filling you up with a twinge of wonder. Where is this ride going?

Suddenly your neck snaps backward at a whopping ninety-eight-degree angle, and a rush comes over you—adrenaline, joy, fear. Before you even realize it, you are chugging up to the very tippy top, the one place you always longed to be. Then, in a single moment, whoosh! You are on the bottom again. The ride is over in minutes, and you want to go back—you anticipate going back. It's all about the anticipation of the rise up, the slow build of excitement, and the sudden whoosh on the way down.

But the truth is, almost everything is in the anticipation, not in the actual action. The actual ride ends up being some kind of disappointment. It never lasts as long as you want it to. It's risky. It makes you nervous.

That's how I feel about growing up so far. It's never what I had hoped for, and that makes me angry. I never wanted to grow up anyway! I'm disappointed about what has happened. I have tried to listen and react, really I have, but the resulting adolescence is nothing like what I hoped for.

I like to think that there will always be someone around to help us in and out of the roller coaster. Sometimes that means parents, who help strap you in and show you where to sit. Sometimes it's friends, who ride and scream on the ride with you. Sometimes it's just you, all by yourself, figuring out how to start the machine.

Whatever the case, we're riding it constantly. We're stuck in perpetual motion and have no idea where the ride stops. Or do we?

Jake

January 17

Me and Kevin went down to the beach today for no reason. It was pretty nice because even though there's still a lot of snow on the ground, the beach was still sandy. Down by the beach there's this deserted amusement park area too. It's small, like more of a carnival. We wished it was open.

Actually we were supposed to go buy snowboards, but we never did. I bought *Snowboarder* magazine instead. Later on when we drove home, we just went over to the Morans' house and played N64. We do a lot of that lately. Then we went to Jonny's and played more cards like always too. That's what winter is about. Playing games and just hanging out. No place to really go, I guess.

Kevin

It's Monday, which is ok but I really do wish it still were the wkend b/c me & Jake went to the beach & looked at a bunch of kick-ass snowboards it was a great time just goin for the hell of it. Too bad they were too expensive so we couldn't buy any ummm like that took all day almost and we got home around 4 o'clock later in the afternoon or so. Then during the nite we went over to meet Mick Lazlo & the other Mick and also Jonny & played cards & shit I lost more money than before. And as for today, I'm just like hangin here now but the truth is all day has been such a huge drag I am not into going to school anymore, it's something different now. I need to say some more prayers for this. I need to have a better attitude about this shit and fast. Today I just moped and moped. Except actually, life guarding was fun & we did more back boarding too. I wanna be strong 4 all the girls yesssss! Ha ha ta ta

Katie

January 18
@ 10:35 P.M.

Skiing yesterday was so great! Definitely one of the best experiences I've had with Brad so far. We put

85

on our new ski gear—me and my rental skis—and signed up for a lesson together. Brad didn't need one, but he said he wanted to stay with me. It was only my 2nd time skiing and it was so nice of him to stay. He could have been skiing the double diamonds all day. There were a few hills when he would grab me and I felt so safe in his arms! He only dropped me once but swore he'd never do it again. We got home after 9 last night.

And now today we're off from school. It's Martin Luther King Day. I'm doing a lot of schoolwork to catch up and then Brad and I are going to the movies later. In just a few more months my hardest high school year will be over!!!

Baxter

January 18

NO SCHOOL!!!

I am definitely bored. Oh well.

In English we're supposed to be starting *The Great Gatsby* so I went to the store and bought a copy today with my mom. It's by F. Scott Fitzgerald. He's supposed to be good. That's what Teresa said.

Later on Derek is coming over to play N64 and hang out. I am so glad he and I are still good friends even though we don't see that much of each other.

He's one of my oldest and best friends. I met Derek in kindergarten when he was using blocks and I was acting like a frog. I jumped into his tower and he thought that was cool. We usually get along fine except when he sleeps over. By the end of those nights he usually says something racist and it pisses me off. He can make me laugh other times. I just don't like him putting down other people for no reason. But he still can make me laugh.

Emma said maybe she'd call later. I think I'll call her first. Maybe we can go to the mall or to Vito's for a slice.

Emma

I got my period yesterday and I just hate this time of the month. It's extra hard because I don't wear tampons, I only wear pads. I just don't know why but every time I use tampons it's just so painful so I don't wear them. Other people think I'm crazy but I don't care because I'm more comfortable the other way. Oh who knows, I just want the next 6 days to be over already! I'm so sick of feeling sick and moody.

By the way I am still totally pissed at Roger for all the shit he was giving me about the semi. I don't really care what happens at this point. And along with everything else I get this note today in class from

Sherelle, which is like totally out of nowhere like what is this supposed to mean. Maybe I am just feeling bitchy, but she is like only into herself these days. All she ever talks about is sex.

Like in this note Sherelle sent, it's about this guy Miguel we know who apparently has a girlfriend at Joyce but who hooked up w/someone else over the weekend, like they had sex. Ok so I know that's interesting to some people but then she said that she and I should have a 3-way with this guy, like she was joking I know. She always says shit like that about sex w/like all the guys in school blah. And of course that's just gross I think. She says I seem kinda quiet lately and is something wrong w/Cliff. She says she wants to go hang out but she is always way too busy. And of course she was worrying about what she should get Bobby for Valentine's Day already, which I think is just stupid. I'm not worried about Cliff at all. Sherelle's changed or something. One good thing is at least she wasn't going off on me like she used to. Oh whatever. I can't deal with her problems right now. I have enough of my own. I have such bad cramps I swear I could get sick!!!!

Billy

Okay so even though I'm back at school I had a good weekend—5 days off thanks to the snow days and MLK Day. It was good that we had off yesterday especially b/c I needed it to recover from this big-ass party we had Sunday night at this girl Jennifer's house.

So this girl Jennifer is friends w/Lexi, who is my teammate Deke's gf. And of course Deke is like one of my best friends. Now obviously this is a *very good* thing cause I meet all these hot girls through him. And last nite was no exception, of course. Beer, beer, and yes more beer. Like 15 of us kids were in this little house and then we all slept over in big piles. It was great.

The thing is that more than drinking or driving I feel lately the need to interact and meet some new people. I mean I don't have to like everyone just to hang out w/them, just socializing is the important part, essential to life happiness. Most of the kids from this area and the other towns near us who I'd never met were there at Jennifer's place. And I got to know some people and laugh and that's the important thing. I laughed my ass off.

Jake

What a joke life is these days—it's worse than before. My grades have started to go down and I actually found out that I just failed part of the reading test for the HSPTs. I have to retake it. I must take a basic skills class so I can prepare again and do better. At least I get a second chance. I found out earlier than everyone else because my guidance counselor pulled me into her office and told me. She figured I should know before the letter went home to my parents. She knows how things are at home these days. I appreciate that.

At least I'm feeling happy about prom this year. Rebecca Rinaldi asked me already and I said yes the other day. She really is a hottie and I would like going w/her because she is also a good dancer and I love dancing. I am happy with this decision. Of course another hot girl Nicole who goes to Grimes also asked me, and this other chick who is an okay dancer, her name is Angie and she has big tits. Three girls is good news for me in the middle of everything else. I think I'll go with Rebecca still.

Teresa

Dear Diary,

Yesterday, before I started my new job @ KidCare, I got some really bad news. I have to get all 4 of my wisdom teeth pulled! My friend tells me that it's the most pain she ever felt in her life, that she got sick from the stuff that puts you to sleep and ended up being out of school from Mon.–Thurs. What will I do? I am sooooo scared!

Other than that, the rest of the day *and* work were absolutely great. I clicked totally w/the people I work with, which surprised me. My boss is very cool. And of course the kids are all totally adorable! After only a few hours working there I already think I have my favorites. One of the kids whose name is Jimmy has a bad case of ADD and he's on all kinds of medication. I feel so bad for him. He can't control himself sometimes and I just want to help him so much! All the kids are so cute and innocent—and the rumble room there brings back sooooo many memories!!

I miss being so young when everything in life was so easy. I never had to worry about *anything* as opposed to now when I have to worry about everything!!!

Katie

January 19
@ 12:18 A.M. (really the 20th, I guess)

We really did a lot in school today—everyone is trying desperately to catch up and in the meantime time is flying by! We already have 4 tests scheduled for the rest of this week. I can't sleep just thinking of it. And today was another rehearsal for the musical. Of course Rachel Ross was there and she is *SUCH* a fake. She has been missing rehearsals because she says she is sick. I don't doubt that she is because she looks pretty bad these days, but it's annoying to me that she comes to school and then not to rehearsal. If I can go to both so can she, right?

I am also having trouble sleeping tonight because it is the anniversary of a *very* important occasion along the progression to maturity for me—and I can't get it off my mind. It was exactly one year ago today that I officially broke up with Robert.

Only 365 days ago I was a complete wreck, which was *horrible*. I know I will always have to see him around JFK and in town, but it feels good knowing that a whole year has passed.

I believe I have made tremendous progress in discovering myself and in expressing the true me to everyone around me. There are *no* boundaries to what I can do or be. I keep telling myself this. There is a quote that I have up on my bulletin board that expresses this perfectly:

No one can predict to what heights you can soar until you spread your wings.

Mom remembered the significance of today too. Of course she went through all the Robert stuff with me so it was an important break for her at the end too. In honor of this, she went shopping and got me a huge surprise. When I came home from rehearsal tonight, she had bought me this gorgeous gown for the prom in this silver color. She had fallen in love w/it and I did too—and I think Brad will too! It's poofy with a bustier top and little embroidered flowers. It looks like an old Victorian gown, actually. I feel like Cinderella when I put it on. I just need glass slippers to match—and Mom says we'll get those too! Gran wants to sew sleeves on though—she thinks the strapless is too much skin showing! Oh well, that's my gran! Actually, Mom and I are going to get the dress fitted soon. I have to go do homework even though it's after 12:00. I think we might have a quiz tomorrow and if you study before you fall asleep you remember *everything* better!

Kevin

1/20

Yesterday sucked at school ohhhh man soooo slow it just doesn't seem to end. Nothing new here as far as that shit goes. I wish I could write about good stuff happening at JFK but I just think lately there is no good stuff for whatever reason like swimming practice was hard b/c we haven't had any practice in like 5 days and I was trying hard too but oh well. After school we went to a meet but the other team was just too freakin good so we lost terribly. We expected to lose though.

There was like one good thing that did happen today oh wait Cristina bought me candy at lunch for no reason at all it made me soo happy. She is the greatest I swear I love her and it kills me not knowing what is happening w/us. Something either will happen or it won't happen but I wish it would just be over with. I wish I knew what was gonna happen in the future w/me & her. It's too messed for me to even think about going to the prom or anything so I think maybe I'll do the friend thing & like go w/Marybeth or May or someone I can hang with. I dunno. Ta ta

Baxter

January 20

In the past few months I have tried to make something happen with Megan. I thought so much about the perfect date we could have. But nothing has happened so far and every time we talk on the phone it's about school. Like today in the hall she smiled at me but then all she wanted to know was what the reading was in English. I guess I should be happy she talks to me about anything, but I'm not.

I talked to her friend Jessica, who I used to like. Jessica says she doesn't know what's going on. She says Megan likes someone but she doesn't know who. I don't believe her but that's okay.

Actually, I am thinking about getting Megan something for Valentine's Day next month. My mom said she would help me pick out something nice. I have been saving up, and it was supposed to be money for my trip to Australia but I can wait for that.

marybeth

January 20th

I still am pissed off about all the shit that went down w/Paulie. He never did come back to get me the other night, not that I really expected he would. It just pisses me off 2 much. After I waited around for a while, I finally did give Lance a call and we went out driving around. It was late but we went n e way. Of course when we were out I made Lance drive by Paulie's house, and his car was right there in the driveway so he definitely blew me off big time. *WHAT A TOTAL DICKHEAD.* That's all I have to say about that. *DICKHEAD!!!!!!!!!!!!!!!!!!*

Oh yeah, the next day I think it was the Monday

we had off I talked to that guy TJ again, the one who plays basketball, and I was happy for like a minute b/c he wanted to come over. Unfortunately 4 me it rained and so he never did. I am having shit luck w/guys. This sucks so much! If I weren't such a wiseass, I might cry about it ha ha.

Yesterday I had a BB game & got called on a flagrant foul b/c I pushed some girl. It was totally an accident though but of course Coach Vozar didn't see it that way. He said I was a total disgrace. He went crazy on me and I came this close to just telling him right there to f-off! This is like the tenth time he and I have had problems. I told TJ what happened and he just told me to blow it off & keep cool. He sez the season is 1/2 over n e way so who cares. Does TJ know how hot he is? I could die.

Oh yeah BTW: Kevin & I decided to go to the prom together. No one else 2 go with. We were laughing about that one.

Billy

1-20

Who the hell am *I* supposed to go to the prom with? I have been talking to this one girl Margret who's a freshman. Actually, Blair D. saw me around with her at the lockers. She gave me real attitude about the whole thing. She just cannot get over me.

Everyone is expected to pick a date now so you can plan. I think I will end up waiting until the very last minute. I mean, I know there are hot girls in my grade or the grade below who would probably go with me, but I don't know anyone I'm really into. Right now I still feel the same as I did at the beginning of the year. I am more into hookups and meeting a lot of different girls from different classes.

Katie

January 21
@ 5:50 P.M.

Today was a weird day—freshman orientation and as I walked around JFK as the Community Club representative, I felt sad and excited all rolled into one. These are the last freshmen (i.e., next year's class) that we'll ever see! I'm starting to get excited already about the fact that next year we move up and we're seniors. I need something to look forward to or I'll stay totally stressed out.

Later this afternoon we had a short Community Club meeting and we were asked to place nominations for the Community Chairman, which is this position of honor for students or teachers. I nominated Miss Shapiro. Baxter couldn't believe it, but I really think it was the right choice. She deserves it for all the time she puts in—without being paid for it. I've already gotten one recommendation and I will write another one. I hope we can get it for her.

I am meeting Brad for dinner in about an hour. He said he has something he needs to talk about. I wonder what's wrong.

Teresa

Jan 21

Dear Diary,

All day in school I went from being hot to cold to sweaty to freezing. There is something really not right about me. My head was pounding and I needed to sleep. I am not kidding, I have not felt this sick in a long, long time. I actually cried in school because I didn't know what I should do about work. I didn't want to go because I felt sooooo crappy, but it's my first week! I can't take any time off on the first week!

But I did. I got home and took 2 Advil, which broke the fever I had. It stopped my headache. But now it's later and I am beginning to feel sick and woozy all over again. I feel like *CRAP*!

Jake

January 22

Well today flew by. Classes were good because all we did was review for midterms that are coming up next Monday. Tonight I went with Jonny to DJ the dance at the middle school down the street. I danced of course because that is what I do. All the little girls love me—one girl who was like in 6th grade wanted to know if I was single. It was so funny. My sister Jill was embarrassed to know me.

After the dance we packed up and went over to Jonny's house. Then Angie came over—she is one of the girls who asked me to the prom. She looked good tonite—she was wearing this tight stretch top that made her look big there. We went to have McDonald's and watched a movie. We then left and took Jonny home and then onto my house. At my house I asked if I could have a good-nite kiss and then me and Angie hooked up and I went inside. Later I went on AOL and went to sleep.

Emma

1/22, 7:05 p.m.

I cannot believe this. Yesterday Mom got a letter in the mail that basically told her I failed one of the sections on the HSPT (High School Proficiency Test) that we took a while ago back in October. I failed the reading section! I was so hysterical because now I have to take this basic skills class with a bunch of idiots. I can't believe it. I am not an idiot. I cried and screamed and basically yelled all last night. I screamed at my mom and told her that there was *NO WAY* I would take that class.

I was such a mess I called Baxter hysterically crying and he had to calm me down. At least he listened to me. He made me feel better. He started saying all these nice things to me and just tried to make me feel better about myself because I was freaking out saying how I would never get into college and would be an idiot forever. He kept saying that I was just overreacting and that I should calm down. I am so glad he was there for me.

It's just that I never expected this to happen. I have been so worried about passing or failing my driving test that I forgot all about this stupid test. I am stupid. I thought maybe I could get out of it somehow, but there's no way. There is nothing else I can do. I did find out that some other of my friends failed and that made me feel a little bit better. I mean I know I am pretty smart and am not a total idiot. Maybe the basic skills class will also help me with my SATs. I guess I got so upset before because I was just very embarrassed. I don't want people to laugh at me.

I told Marybeth, Katie, Baxter, and 2 other people at school about my failing. I was gonna tell Sherelle too but I changed my mind. I'm afraid she will tell everyone at school or something. I'm trying to stay focused on the positive, even though I feel so dumb inside right now. Baxter said to focus on what's good.

One very good thing is Cliff is coming over in a little while after his work gets out. I want to see him so much right now. When he called before I started crying and he sounded all worried about me. Well, he's gonna get more of that tonite. We decided to watch *Dawson's Creek* on tape because we didn't see it on Wednesday nite. I taped it. So now I gotta go and take a shower fast! I want to see him so bad!

Baxter is always right somehow. He told me to keep it together and I would feel better as the night went on. That was good advice. I do feel better already.

Good AdviceGood Advice

Teresa:

The best advice anyone ever gave to me was to totally follow my heart and to strive to be the best I can be no matter who or what tries to stop me. I will listen and believe this advice forever.

Kevin:

This WAS SAid to me At Some point but I leARned it moRe fRom expeRience And thAt is "neveR let Anything Stop you fRom SAying whAt you feel", whetheR it is good oR bAd doesn't mAtteR—you mAy neveR get A Second chAnce And life is too fReAkin ShoRt.

Katie:

My friend and mentor Jaclyn Roome at college says that I should just believe in me and not worry about the future. Of course, I do think that is good advice—it's just hard advice to follow! How can I not worry about the future?

Good Advice Good Advice

Marybeth:

Always go w/your intuition no matter what. It's funny b/c your gut feeling is usually never wrong but it is ignored all the time. If people paid more attention 2 it, things could be better 4 everyone involved.

Baxter:

My friend Derek told me not to overreact and start getting mad at someone until I know the whole story. He always gives the best advice, even if I don't always take it.

Emma:

Be my own person and don't let other people influence me, which of course means stop worrying all the time about what other people are saying. I mean, I know I do worry sometimes but I can't help it. The person who told me that doesn't give a shit what other people think—she just does and says whatever she wants.

Good Advice Good Advice

<u>Billy:</u>
1. Hang tough (my football coach says that).
2. Don't let the turkeys get you down (Lee my brother always says that half joking but it really is true).

<u>Jake:</u>
Always follow your own dreams because someday they'll be someone else's dreams. I don't want anyone to get there before I do.

Kevin

I have had like 3 tests in the last 2 days, 2 today and 1 yesterday. The only thing was shit—I sorta cheated on one of the tests, which is really bad. It was like the first time in my life I have ever done anything like that. It just was too much stuff to remember and I am just superbusy like I had practice until like 9:00 last nite. I made like a mini–cheat sheet and I know for a fact that almost everyone else in the class did the same thing. There's just too much work and with my swim team and other stuff there is never time to do it all don't people understand this? Of course I know it's wrong and I felt way bad about it but whatever, I did it and I guess I'll just have to live with myself. 'Nuf said.

So yesterday's swim meet went better than the last one we met at the pool at Grimes—they are so lucky b/c their pool kicks ass it's sooo nice. Ok so we didn't win in the end but the match was a lot closer so we had more fun. I wasn't that nervous like I am usually when we race this time it was different. I hate being nervous.

Katie

Of course I got all worried the other night and Brad had nothing serious to talk about in the end of it all. Well, it was serious, but nothing bad. He is just so sweet and thoughtful! He just wanted to tell me that he loved me again. And he wanted to pick the right moment. He does that sometimes to me lately. He sets me up and then proceeds to talk about the future. The only problem with that is I don't always know what I see in my future. But for right now, he is just perfect for me. I do know that.

Today everything else felt perfect too. Mom had bought me that beautiful prom dress and today we went to the mall store so I could get fitted properly. It's a little big so they recommended I get a size smaller, only the store didn't carry it. They have to order it from another store in Las Vegas of all places! It was so funny trying it on. Everyone in the store came over to me and was hovering around saying, "You look like Cinderella. . . ." I don't want to stand out, but I do love this gown. I am so lucky that my mom found it just for me!

Baxter

I really hate the fact that I care about what other people think. I care way too much. I was on the phone tonight with Katie. She said that apparently Megan Randall might be going to the prom with some other guy. But she said she doesn't know that for sure. She only heard it somewhere. And all I can think about now is Megan and some mystery guy. And what if he's a senior. That would suck if he was older than me.

Tonight Mom made me a lot of food that I like. It cheered me up. We had buffalo wings and macaroni.

I also listened to my Britney CD, which cheered me up even more. I still think Britney is soooo incredibly *HOT*! Someone told me she is going to be going on tour this summer. I have to get tickets. I put up the poster from the CD and she's the first person I see every day.

Teresa

Jan 23

Dear Diary,

I feel much better than I did the other day *THANK GOD*. I am glad because tonite me & Gina hung out with these 4 senior guys from JFK: Grant, Keith,

Christopher, and Joe. We've only talked to them before, but never really hung out. But since we weren't doing anything and it's Saturday (my mom would be soooo happy!) we decided to let them take us out. They picked us both up and then we just drove around for hours trying to find something to do. Finally we went back to this one guy Keith's house and just watched a movie. It was cool being w/them because all 4 of them have such distinct personalities:

Keith is cute, smart, down-to-earth, and witty. He's just an awesome, funny, great guy.

Christopher is more the quiet type but when he does talk he is totally hysterical!

Joe likes me, which is cool, but we're just friends and I wanna keep it that way. He likes to joke around and tease people a lot but he has a huge heart.

Grant likes Gina and he is as dumb as dirt! Don't get me wrong—he's really fun to be with and all that it's just that he is kind of stupid and tells pointless stories. And obviously, Gina doesn't like Grant in the way he likes her, but on the whole all that doesn't matter. We still had a really fun time together and said we should all hang out more often.

It's always sooooo good to expand your horizons to meet different people, to hang out with a different crowd, especially since most of our friends are off with their boyfriends. But that's their problem!

Billy

My computer is very fucked up and it's been that way since the beginning of January. I can't send or get any e-mails, which is no good. I just don't understand what the problem is. My dad said I probably did something to the computer because I'm always messing w/it but that is just not true. It sucks though because I miss talking online.

Yesterday I got my varsity jacket and it has the school logo plus a letter for football and another letter for lacrosse on each of the arms. It's phat and I am so proud to wear it. I am going to wear it every single day.

For the past few months all I have been thinking about is playing lacrosse. It is no question my favorite sport. I think practices start already this week on Wednesday. I'm not sure. I am also trying to get in shape in other ways too like running every day after school. Jake's on the team w/me too, but he doesn't have much free time these days.

Jake

January 23

I went to work and got 5 leads today. Then I went home and did shit for the whole day until like 7:00

when Jonny came by and got me. We went back to his place and played cards and started drinking.

It was mad fun—who was there were some girls like Pam, Deb, and Randi, who I know pretty well, and then 2 other girls who I hang out with less, Amy Flanagan and Suzie Wells, who are part of this group at school that everyone calls The Mix. Okay so I hooked up with both Amy and Suzie. Amy just broke up with her boyfriend and then Suzie told me she kind of broke up w/hers too. That's what she said.

Kevin was there too and he hooked up w/Randi for like the whole nite. And then Mick Geffen hooked up with Amy and Suzie too and he is still going out with his girl. That was kind of shitty I think but whatever—we were having fun times. Then everyone played strip poker and started playing with those sexual dice that I got. We were playing for a while. Jonny ended up hooking up with Amy and Suzie both too. Of course a lot more than hooking up went on in some cases, but I don't want to say what. It was *definitely* mad fun.

Kevin

1/24

Today at like 1:00 me, Mick, Mick, and Jake went over to Jonny's b/c it is his b-day and he's 17 now all we did was just chill & play some cards (I broke even wahoo) um and we just screwed around basically the rest of the day sucked.

But some real shit happened last night ok me & Micky Lazlo & his gf Deb had to go to this Sweet 16 for a little. Ok so then after that happened, we went to pick up Cristina and head over to Jonny's again. We had plans to play cards and hang loose, again b/c it's his b-day and we were celebrating early. So then everything was pretty chill and cool when all of a sudden The Mix walks in and we were like "shit" & I didn't know them that well but I guess I thought it was cool, I mean we're friends and all that. So this is good I was thinking real good.

Ok then all hell broke loose like it all went down starting w/me & my friend Randi were just sitting there just talkin about how she & her man Daniel were fighting and how she is prob. just gonna break up w/him anyway b/c all he ever talks about doin is having sex. So then I notice the way she's sitting and how she's tryin to kiss me all afterward and while we're talkin and then we DID kiss and I'm like you really should stop you really shouldn't do this. Ok and she's like I know, I know, but I've wanted to and I don't care about Daniel anymore b/c he's just a dickhead anyway and I'd rather be w/a sweet guy like you. So now we start hooking up for the whole nite.

In the meantime me, Micky G., and this other chick Louise who I don't know so well we start playin strip poker till she's in her underwear all of a sudden acting like she thought she knew how to play the game but we know she doesn't know jack shit so we stop the game right there b/c she sucks at it.

Ok then later I see Jake and Jonny over on the other side of the room and they're hookin up like a mad # times w/Amy and Suzie Wells who is really really hot ok. Then I'm like what is going on around here b/c Micky G. suddenly hooks up w/Suzie too. Only w/Mick she did it all and he's like shitting his pants b/c he knows his gf will find out what happened and I am just sittin there thinking what a stupid shit he is for doing that w/her. It was seriously like a massive fucking orgy in there goin on and now Louise hates Amy & Suzie b/c they were both kissing someone she wanted for sooo long. In the end Micky G. told his gf all about his problem and she knows. Meanwhile Suzie's bf doesn't really care what she does, which is def. a f-up thing I think. They broke up last nite b4 it all happened I guess. And that's the whole story from me who was there some weird shit happening. Ta ta

Jake

January 24
Today me and Kevin and the two Micks and Jonny were just chilling since it's Jonny's 17th birthday. We had pizza and cake. We hung out and played cards. We talked about what happened last night and said who the fuck cares. It is now in the past.

When I got home from Jonny's place, I stayed up

talking w/my older brother Nate. He told me some sick shit. The thing is Geffen's gf happens to be Nate's girlfriend's sister. I think she knows what happened with him and Suzie yesterday night. I think she *KNOWS* maybe that they did it. Nate said that Geffen and his girl were fighting all day and it was ugly.

p.s. I didn't get Jonny a present yet but I will soon. He's getting his license tomorrow.

Marybeth

January 24th

I can't believe how bored I am. I haven't felt like doing n e thing. Right now I'm on the phone w/TJ tho & boy oh boy oh boy do *I WANT HIM*! He called last nite too. I think we may hang out this weekend. I hope we do. TJ is such a hottie I can't stop thinking about him!

BTW: My exams have been going ok. I'm happy @ that. It's about time.

Oh yeah, yesterday I did not play in my basketball game *again*. That pisses me off 2 much. I was the only 1 who didn't play too. But I will stick w/it. I know if I stick w/it that'll prob. piss off Coach Vozar more than anything.

I'm sorta tired now. Gotta go.

Baxter

January 24

My dog Coconut has been acting really down lately. She's in bad shape. We were worried because for the last few days she doesn't want to eat. Now it's been like 10 days and she still hasn't eaten. My dad and mom and me took Coconut and went over to the emergency room at the clinic. The vet tried to help. He said her stomach has an ulcer or a growth inside. She was in pain. I am worried.

I really love my dog.

Coconut

Emma

1/24, 4:15 p.m.

I wish Baxter were home so we could study for this stupid test on Tuesday. I just got out of the shower and I am sitting here in my bed worrying about it. It's a chem midterm and it's like so important for our grade. There is so much information and he told us absolutely nothing. I also have an Italian class midterm tomorrow afternoon but I'm less worried about that one. I can study for that after dinner tonight. Anyway me and Marybeth and Baxter all sit near each other so we can probably cheat if we have to. We always can but we usually don't need to because she is such an easy teacher. She doesn't make exams hard at all. I think she even knows we cheat because how could she not know. I mean, we are always like talking to each other during the tests. We're helping each other with the answers right there in front of her.

I am still getting over everything that happened last night it was a real eventful night. I was supposed to hang out with Marybeth and Sherelle but neither of them beeped me. I don't know what's going on there. So then I went out with my cousin Barb and my friend Karen instead and we went to hang out at this guy she knows Tommy's house. Okay so his house was like in the middle of nowhere and Karen ended up driving around for like more than 40 minutes before we got there when it was supposed to be like 10 minutes away. He gave us bad directions. And then when we walked in Tommy was like what happened and Karen just went off on him it was really out of hand. We hoped we were going to see Tommy and go to the movies but it got too late all of a sudden. We were pissed. Karen was even more pissed than me.

Okay so then it was late and then I came home to find my sister Lynn on the phone with *my* boyfriend

Cliff, which made me so mad. She was really talking with his friend Josh, but whatever. All I know is that I tried to get on the phone with Cliff and he was like I can't talk now me and Josh are talking to Lynn. It was like he blew me off and then he started laughing. Whatever. He was being a jerk. And I know he was messed up too. He was drinking a lot last night of course. I flipped out on my sister though she was such a bitch about the whole thing. She grabbed the phone back and everything. Sometimes she acts like she is just too cool for everyone. So finally I went to bed around 2:00 A.M. I wasn't feeling that good.

I woke up at 10:30 and wanted to call Cliff right away but I didn't. He was probably still sleeping. But we talked later on. Actually, it turns out he was awake in the morning and he was puking his guts out all night. I guess his mom caught him doing it because there was this crash when something fell in the bathroom while he was puking and it made a loud noise. Of course Cliff was like really drunk so he doesn't even know what his mom said to him at that point. He was telling me all this today and he was very upset about all of it.

I can't believe Cliff would get caught that is so dumb because now his mom might ground him and then who knows when I'll see him. He said his parents were mad but that they weren't yelling they were ignoring him. That's how he could tell how mad they were. They wouldn't say anything. I hope they all talk soon. I have to see him at least one of these days! I

116

dunno I'll have to wait and see what they say. He's upset about getting caught it's all he can talk about.

I am so glad I wasn't there. If I had been there, his mom would hate me now.

I told Cliff I get my license in 10 days and then I will be able to take him places.

I miss him already.

Emma+Cliff ♡ ♡

Katie

Brad just called to wish me luck on my midterms this week. This is definitely going to be a week from hell.

This school is so stupid. Normal kids get to go into school for midterm exams and then go home. JFK, on the other hand, makes us take a 2-hour exam every day and then stay in school for the rest of the day and have other tests and homework during the *same week*! Things are really crazy already and it's only Tuesday! I'm really trying to remember lately that life is not just about grades. But I do hope my grades don't suffer at all this marking period or go down from last time. This is such an important time. Unless something really drastic happens this week, these are the grades I will get:

117

AP English B+ (possibly A-)

AP history A!!!! (up from a B last semester!)

Choristers A+

Math B- (I'm *really* nervous about this exam so I'm underestimating the grade)

Advanced chemistry Hopefully a B+ (I understand it a little better now)

Photog. A+

So basically I have kept up and maybe even improved (cross my fingers) my GPA and things with rehearsals for *The Boy Friend* are going very well! I am now officially halfway through junior year!

Kevin

1/25

Today was um not too good no b/c of many things ok.

First off there are midterms all week and that is not good well actually I'm good until Wed., which is when I have chem and I am just gonna fail that sooo whatever I won't study massively hard I won't care too much at all, why should I?

Ok second thing is the whole thing that happened this wkend. Last night I guess Mick G. called the guy who is going w/that girl Suzie from The Mix. She was the one who messed w/Jake, Jonny, and then Mick. And that was such a crappy thing to do it totally like screwed over Jake and Jonny. Then Jonny called

Geffen back and told him off and said he had ruined his whole 17th b-day and basically leaned on Mick really really hard. So everyone's all depressed now and even today at school Mick G. was threatening Jake and Jonny in the hall like in front of everyone. It is bad bad and everyone says it's just b/c Mick is pissed but I have a bad feeling when everyone is fighting back & forth when we used to be so tight ok.

Ok for me nothing has happened w/Randi who I was with this wkend. Her bf doesn't know anything & I don't think she'll say anything about bein w/me so I don't really care anymore. I just wish the whole thing was over with and never mentioned again cause Randi was like so misleading beyond belief. I will be so so so pissed if anything comes out I will totally blame her it'll be like the worst ever!!!

Only good thing happening is that Jonny got his license today, which is *very cool* for him even with all the other shit going on ok. Ta ta

My Worst Fight Ever

Billy:

One time I got in this fight with Deke but it was nothing really. We were set up by this girl at a party. It was like we both wanted her. I don't remember. I just know we stopped talking for like a week and that flipped me out. Being mad w/each other sucks.

Teresa:

At the beginning of the year I had that fight with Stephanie who I thought was like my BFF! It was one of those awful fights where you both just kinda ignore each other and don't speak. Except we didn't speak for months. She was saying things to people about how I was trying to break up her and her bf, which was wrong. Why would she be dumb enough to think that when I have been her friend my whole life? If we are ever in the same room now we still just catfight. We hardly speak.

My Worst Fight Ever

Jake:

No fights with my friends but sometimes with my mom. Like we fight about me going out. I got mad once and said I hated her and went to my room. She was really upset. I said I was sorry and then we made up.

Katie:

It's so weird because the worst fight ever was definitely last year about Robert. Ironically, I used to fight with my mom about him. Then I ended up fighting with him and against him too. It was so bad all around. I was angry inside and outside.

Baxter:

I will let someone know if I am mad but we both get over it. What's the big deal anyway?

Marybeth:

Ok one time someone beeped my buddy Lance w/143, which is fuck you, and he accused me of doing it! Of course I didn't

My Worst Fight Ever

do it but he got soooo mad at me 4
nothing! But I was like ok that's cool b/c
he apologized & he knew he was wrong & the
fight ended.

Emma:

I can get mad pretty easy like if
someone pisses me off for no good reason
I will just go off. I think fighting really
bothers me though, like if my parents do
I hate that. I have stupid fights with
Cliff like all the time but we still love
each other!

Kevin:

Ooooh mAn where do I stARt
fighting like w/Neil like At Disney
oR mAybe my pARents like if they
don't tRust me I cAn just get
so mAd At them yeah my fAmily is
the woRst eveR! BAsicAlly I tRy
hARd not to fight though And tRy
to keep it All good bet. me & my
fRiends.

Teresa

Dear Diary,

Tonight my dad picked me up from KidCare & took me directly to a local hockey game. It was *AWESOME*!!! The Rockets won 4–1. My dad's boss got him the tickets and we had seats in the front row!!!! I love hockey so much. I think next year I want to be a hockey manager. I have to remember to talk to Emma about that since she does it now!

When the teams came out to the ice I was right there watching. I love everything about hockey especially the players! I always have and I always will!!! I found out that the Rockets practice at the same rink as the Redwood Reds sometimes. *THAT'S* soooooooo awesome!!! I told my dad we have to go.

By the way, I wrote a new poem. My new job inspires me sooo much!

TUGGING AT MY HEART

There's a pull at my jeans
And a glance my way
An anxious face, small and round,
An anxious plea that comes to say,
"Come chase me!" She speaks
Laughing, playing as I smile back.
Of course I smile at her
And all I can say is, "Sure."
She makes me grin, she fills me up

And makes my heart leap.
Every day there is a smile on my face,
For every child in the place.
They take nothing for granted like you and me
They take simple stones and make a city
Using their imaginations without rest
Being all they can be, this isn't a test.
I think we don't see children like we should,
So much more sweet, smart, and good.
But sooner or later they will part
They will grow up and move away from me.
At the very least have I touched one heart?
And how have I let their hearts touch me?

—T. J. F.

Oh—today was my AP history midterm exam and we had to write 2 essays. I actually didn't finish one of them and now I am scared that I did poorly on the whole test. I hope not. Better go study for my next test!!

Marybeth

January 26th

I'm so tired of studying. Midterms are horrible. Right now I am actually on the phone w/TJ. Oh my gosh today we were supposed to meet each other again during class, but my teacher wouldn't let me out 2 see him! I almost got into a fight w/her about it.

Jeez, do I want TJ baaaaaaad! He is 2 cool, like the funniest person to talk to. He said maybe we should hang out this Friday but I dunno if we will.

TJ is so *HOT*!

I wonder if anything will ever come out of this 4 me. I'm waiting. . . .

Baxter

January 27

Since last Sunday we've been holding off to see what's going on with the dog. Well we found out today that Coconut has been *real* sick.

Her uterus was filling with poison and they had to take it out before it exploded. So she had to have emergency surgery. She had the surgery and now she's at home recovering. The worst part is that they shaved off her fur like all over her body and now she's funny looking. I hope she gets better fast. *I LOVE MY DOG!!!!*

I got a call from Megan today. I didn't call her back though. She probably just wanted me to help her study for exams. Speaking of which, I have to go study more for midterms *RIGHT NOW*. Bye!

Emma

Happy Anniversary to me + Cliff!!!

So now it's been two months for me and Cliff and everything is going good. Like last night we had this phone conversation that made me so happy. I can't explain it, we were just fooling around and making fun of each other it was great. The only bad thing lately is my worrying about getting my license. I am so so so nervous. Only 7 more days. If I don't pass I will cry. Even worse, I will die.

I am in a pretty good mood today because I found out that I got an A on my Italian exam this week and a B+ on chemistry. I hoped to do well since I studied for like 6 hours or more. By the end of Monday night I was ready to kill myself but all the studying really paid off. This will help a lot with my marking period grades. I hope I will get an average of like a B+ that will make me happy. I am thinking I might get an A in math too, which is very good and better than last year at this time. My next exam isn't until Friday and that's history. I have to study even though I heard it was pretty easy. Tonight I have to go to a hockey game first though. Maybe I can study after but I dunno. Whatever. The only test right now I am afraid of is my driving test, like I said. I hope so much that I pass! I hope so!

Jake

Yesterday and today were basically the same ol, same ol. All my classes are boring because we are in the middle of exams. Yesterday I went to life guarding and did the usual. Now in English we are reading *The Great Gatsby*. The story of the book is interesting but reading it is hard to understand. I don't understand when we start talking about the symbolism in it.

Today I had my chemistry exam. It was a little hard. I hope the others are easier. Later on at work tonite I got a bonus. It was a surprise from my boss. I love my job because I am having fun with my friends, talking on the phone, and getting paid at the same time.

Katie

January 28
@ 6:45 P.M.

We had a rehearsal tonight but we left early because of exams. I am so relieved that this week is almost over!

I am really enjoying this year so far. It's funny—I was talking to my friend Carlos about friendships and how I finally realized that the popular kids are not always the ones who are liked. The true respect goes to a kid who leads, who does not stray from his or her goals and who is not totally influenced by the actions of others. Carlos agreed with me and then Brad also said something later on about how in freshman and sophomore year he thought success was just about who you hung out with and which parties you went to and what kind of car you drove. He said that he never had a clue about what he wanted and that it was *me* who showed him how what he was thinking wasn't true at all. Brad says he didn't have any idea what he wanted until he met me. Then he told me I had this huge impact on his whole life. *WOW!*

I mean, Brad was never a bad guy, it's not like I totally changed him or something, but I do think he tends to follow the crowd when it comes to stuff like his drinking activities. He says that because of me he now sees how maybe it's okay not to drink and that you can gain much more respect by holding strong to your goals and not just following everyone else.

Billy

1-28

Everyone has this Word upgrade software I want for my computer! It's like a publishing program or something and I want it now! My parents just don't get it. I am about to be completely left out of what's going on around me. I don't have any of the computer games, my e-mail is fucked up still. I just need to really get it together fast.

Oh yeah, I think I aced most of my exams. I knew I would. They were so easy compared to last year. Things just seem easier to me these days. I am enjoying a nice cold Coke right now and studying chemistry and listening to my old Boyz 2 Men CD. These guys have great voices. Rehearsal for the musical was canceled tonite, by the way. They only had us come pick up the music and sing some warm-ups just to connect. It'll be a good show guaranteed. Okay, 4 exams down. 1 to go.

Kevin

1/28

Hey um it's Thursday and the week is almost over ok well I had 90 min. of gym, which I hate more than anything else in the world b/c of the teacher Mr. Frankel, who has bad breath and likes getting me to get in trouble. Ok yesssss how can I forget the boring midterms too? The rest of classes are doing *NOTHING* good since the tests take up like most of the days around here sooo that's what.

Ok so yesterday Wed. I had that chem exam & I thought it would be hard but I didn't wanna study for it but anyway it wasn't so bad, not deadly. But anyway I got a B- on it so what can you do? And considering some of the rest of the grades in the class I was doin ok yeah then nothing else stupendous happened in school not really except um outside the school on Tues. there was a big-ass fight between these students seniors and some local kids who were wailing on the JFK kids it was a bad scene all over but then it passed. Tonite I had swimming so I missed the action really I was doing sprints in the pool and running and I am really tired.

Oh yeah one more thing now I found out this week that everyone knows I secretly want to be w/Cristina, who I was sorta tryin to put out of my mind but I can't. I think I was even thinking of her last wk. when I was hooking up w/Randi and the other girls in The Mix ok yeah so I do I do want Cristina pretty bad. And we kid all the time sure but I still say we'd better stay friends. Ta ta

p.s. Tonite on *Dawson's Creek* it was like my fave episode ever b/c it was about the kid Pacey not getting & giving positive comments from his dad and stuff like that. It was sad and a part of me related to him & his character.

Marybeth

January 29th
Tonite I hung out w/a buncha friends including TJ! We didn't hook up or anything, but we had fun. I

was like teasing TJ saying hey like when r we gonna hook ↑ but I was joking. He was like don't worry, MB, we will. It was cute!

But I think he's putting me on. It's kinda funny how we r when we're together. Oh well what can u do, right? Other than that goin on, I have still been hearing bad rumors about me & that kid Lance, my buddy. I dunno someone thinks we're like together and is saying that all over school. I think maybe it's Rick Wright again. He's still not over me. I don't understand what's goin on. I'll tell you what's goin on: *NOTHING!!*

BTW, I got this letter today in class from Emma. She wuz bored!

marybeth,   1/29

Hey babe what's up? I am so bored in math right now. I have 20 min. left and nothing to do so I am writing you this note. Lucky you! Last nite at SAT prep, that girl Gwen walked in (you know Gwen, who we saw @ that party this year & who dissed Sherelle last summer—that Gwen). Anyway, she walked right into our room and Sherelle was sitting there right next to me and she made this mean-ass face like she was saying get out. I was

like settle down, Sher. Class sucked of
course because all we really did was take
a test for 3 hrs. I think maybe I'll come
to your game today. I don't know. I wish
Cliff could hang out too but I think his
parents still won't allow him out. He said
he will be, but I think he's just joking
with me. He was saying that he needs to
get his ass over to the mall because it's
my birthday coming up. And then I smiled
and told him I already had a valentine for
him. He freaked on me (j/k of course) he
was like oh why don't I just sign my
paycheck over to you.

Do you think I will pass my driver's
ed test? I can't tell you how worried I
am I have been worried like this all week
long. Isn't that just crazy? I'm trying
not to think about it. Oh I have hockey
tonite. wanna come to the game?
whatever if you do or don't. Have you
talked to TG lately? what's going on with
him? Oh well I am gonna stop writing now
because I think the bell is about to ring.
Talk to ya later! ♥ ya!

Em

132

Emma cracks me up. Ouch my throat hurts. I hope I am not sick that would suck. I'm so beat. Bed 4 me!

Teresa

Dear Diary,

I am sooooo excited! 2 months or something ago I met this *really* cute guy at a hockey game, this guy Jesse. He was nice enough. Anyway, last nite we hung out together. I saw him because he's friends w/Wendy's boyfriend so we "double-dated" I guess you could say. We went to the movies. He's pretty cute or he was cute last nite. The only problem is that he tries to go too far when we're in the movie theater. I mean, I have morals, right? Apparently he doesn't. So we did hook up and had a good time. We just didn't go quite as far as I think maybe he wanted to.

I was thinking today about the fact that I haven't seen my brother in a very long time, we always come home at different times and we end up not seeing each other. Even though Vincent and I never ever talk about anything, I still would like to know he's around. Is that weird of me to think that and feel that way? I don't know anymore.

Onto a totally different subject: My work is *AWE-SOME*. I love it sooooo much. I got paid a lot for the last 2 weeks, which is totally good because I feel like I don't deserve that much. I would do this job for *FREE*! That's how much I love it.

Yeah, but I'm still glad it's the weekend!!

Emma

1/29, 11:55 p.m.

I just walked in the door from school. It's Friday thank God.

My history exam went really easy today. The only hard part on it was this graph, which I didn't totally understand. I just kind of guessed at those parts. I guessed at like 6 questions. Oh and my last essay was a little bit short too because I was starting to run out of time. I hope I did well still. I want a B again for the marking period.

Even though it's Friday I unfortunately have to babysit. The lady I do it for called me up and wanted me to do it tomorrow too and I just said I couldn't. I actually can't. We have a hockey game I have to manage. It's busy right now for us. There really isn't anything going on tonite anyway. Well, I was thinking of going to Marybeth & Sherelle's game but I'm not going anymore now. I mean, it really wasn't anything big so I don't feel guilty about not going. We really didn't have any plans after the game either. Marybeth told me she might go out with this guy TJ and I am SURE Sherelle will be going out w/Bobby.

The good thing about babysitting with this woman

is that she pays really well, like $25 for 2 hours, which is good. All I have to do is put the baby to sleep and then wait for the older kid to get tired. She really trusts me with her kids. The other good thing is that I can use her computer and phone while I'm there. She doesn't mind at all. So I can call Cliff when I get there.

p.s. 5 more days and I get my license and I am more nervous than I have been the whole time. I mean, what if I get some asshole guy or some bitchy woman and they decide to just fail me right there for no reason. Ok I know everyone said it's easy but I am just, "Fine." I just have to stop at all the stop signs and use my blinker. My dad is taking me parallel parking again this week too. I can use the practice. I just have to stop thinking about it!!!!

Billy

1-29

I cnt believe this has hapnd to me Rt now I am typing on the cmpter with only one arm. I fellyester-day in lacrose and fuckd up my sholdr soooooo bad. Im making so many spellin mistaks bc I am not used to typinhg with my lft hand and fingres 1 more things the doctr says I have a dislOcated shoulder cant play lacrosse for 3 wlks I am in a lot of pain now so I will say good night I m out.

135

Kevin

1/29

Hey hey hey it's Sat. night. Nonono it's Fri., oh my bad. I can't believe like that's some serious shit that happened to Billy yesterday on the lacrosse field. Jake told me that Billy's shoulder like popped out of the socket, which is gross I am soooo glad I wasn't there to see that.

Today in school it wasn't too bad um I got like a D on some test but LOL I might be able to boost it to a C but who cares right now I don't remember what else happened cause it's late and I am kind of shit-faced right now um I went to a friend's party and since Jonny can drive now he took me home so I love it he's the bomb no but really I am really drunk LOL I had a big-ass screwdriver and beer. It was so freakin good not to have to worry tonite about drivin or not it was like a really freeing experience fm. how I have felt lately about the whole drinking & driving thing.

Billy:

It's hard to think about freedom w/out thinking of the opposite. I feel the opposite more these days. My dad is always pulling this power trip on me about the car, for example. He definitely wants to get in the way of my freedom.

Teresa:

Well, don't we all wish we could be completely free! I think we're at the age where freedom is most important. Right now all of my friends and I think that we can do whatever we want and don't deserve to be told what to do. I think personally that right now freedom may sound appealing, but I don't think it will be that great when we have no one to wash our clothes and cook us our meals.

Freedom Freedom

Baxter:

I have learned to accept that freedom is a good thing, but a very large responsibility. In order to keep freedom, you cannot screw up.

Katie:

I am allowed freedom because my parents trust me completely. I get to go nearly wherever I want within reason and am provided with the necessary funds to do so. I want to have a diverse amount of experiences, and the freedom my parents give me enables me to do just that.

marybeth:

Ok lately my mom has been kinda harsh questioning who I hang w/so she's been stricter, but when she is into my friends she trusts me w/more freedom. It just happens step by step when u get ur license and so on, like as you're maturing.

Freedom Freedom

Jake:

I LOVE IT!! Freedom is great. I love being in charge and out of the house and away from all the rules.

Emma:

My parents give me some freedom but not like a lot. They always have to know where I am and who I am with and all of that crap. I just wish my mom would trust me and know that I won't get myself in trouble and I will make the right decisions. I think it's real important for a teenager to have freedom.

Kevin:

I love freedom believe me AfteR All my f-ups with RelAtionships I like being fRee now And hAving time to do whAt I wAnt being fRee And just chilling And All, not AlwAys

Freedom Freedom

hAving someone know where I Am going or whAt I Am doing And I like my cAr best. A lot of times the best wAy to get freedom is to just drive AwAy.

Baxter

January 30

Midterms have really been tough. I've been studying forever and I still haven't done good. In English I
got the lowest grade on my test all semester and I feel
like such an idiot. I need an A on my essay to even
get a B as the final class grade. Then on chem I studied for like 5 hours or something. I got a B-. He said
that was good. I don't think so at all though. What is
happening to my grades? What is going on inside this
brain of mine?

Last night I went to a party at Derek's house. His
parents were gone away to see his sister off to college, so he had some booze and there was drinking.
Of course I didn't drink. But I did sleep over. It was
a lot of fun to hang out with so many people and
we talked most of the time. The house was a mess.
When I came home I went to sleep for real. What a
week!

p.s. Coconut is recovering nicely from her operation.

Jake

January 30

This week felt so long because of all the exams.
But the tests were easy. And all the other classes that

we had in the meantime were boring because all we did really was sit around waiting for the next test. The only fun thing this week was Thursday. I had auto shop and I fixed my mom's car. I did an oil change on it.

Tonite turned out to be fun. Since now Jonny has his license we can do a lot more like go out because lately Kevin is just so boring. He complains about having to drive all the time. He doesn't like doing it. Jonny is different.

We went over to Derek's for a party and it was all kids from the JFK junior class plus a few sophomores. I drank about 6 Natural Ices and then 1/2 a Budweiser. I was feeling real nice. Kevin got drunk off his ass because he hasn't had a drink in 5 months or something. I was with all of my best friends except for Micky Lazlo, who was with his woman.

People were so drunk and then I went off with Rebecca Rinaldi, who is so hot, but I didn't hook up with her. I had to protect her the whole night. A lot of guys tried to hook up with her but she couldn't control herself and she has a boyfriend so I helped her out. I held her back from doing something she would later regret doing.

After Rebecca left we all just chilled there. It was nice being with everyone like that. Some people slept over but me, Kevin, and Jonny left. I also talked a lot to this other guy Dave Pettit. He is cool and he has some problems at home too so I talk to him about it sometimes. Then we all went home. Jonny was the designated driver. When I got home I went online and to sleep.

Katie

January 30
@ 11:55 P.M.

Last night was crazy and I mean really crazy. Long story. Very long story.

First, Brad took me along to dinner with his family for his brother Karl's birthday. I really didn't want to go—I wanted to go to this party with my friends, but Brad would have felt so out of place without me. He said so. Everyone else in his family was bringing a date. So I went and it was fun for the first part of it. We went for Japanese food, which was surprisingly delicious (I'd never eaten it before). The only problem was that Brad and I got lost driving there! We were in this really run-down neighborhood too, which was pretty scary. But we found the highway again and address.

At dinner I sat down right next to Cindy, Karl's girlfriend. She's Swiss and doesn't have any female friends in America. I think she was going to try to be an au pair but her family fell through. Now she is looking for a job, or *was* looking anyway. We're so close in age, so if she wants to talk or go shopping or just needs a friend I can be here for her. Unfortunately,

I think she needs me more sooner than later. Something really awful happened at the end of the night.

Okay, this is a long story and I am in shock just telling it because it came so suddenly and no one could have predicted anything like this could happen. I know that this was a freaky thing, like a one-in-a-million thing, but it happened.

This morning after I had SAT review and dropped off my little brother and sister to their play group and had lunch with Brad, we decided to go for a drive. Well, as it turns out we called up Karl and Cindy and they decided to go w/us, okay. So there we were driving along to go pick them up, like everything is normal. We pulled into the driveway of the apartment complex where Karl is staying right now and went to ring their bell. The door was open and Cindy was there, lying across the couch. And she was crying— hysterically. So of course we asked what had happened and she told us.

Apparently her dad had been found inside their house in Switzerland and he was dead of carbon monoxide poisoning or something just as strange. He was just found there dead. Cindy was beside herself—she couldn't even speak.

So now Karl and Cindy have decided that they want to fly back to Switzerland for her dad's burial in a couple of days. I am 100% freaked out by the whole story. Brad is so upset and Karl seems really out of it. All Cindy does is cry. I guess she and her dad were close and this is a real shocker. I can't imagine in a million years what it would feel like. I can't imagine.

marybeth

January 30th

I felt like I was really getting it together today. Ok I am home from work. It is now 9:48. I walked in 20 min. ago. But I was better off staying at Shopwell than being here and this is why—my mom is 2 pissed 2 be believed.

Momma sez that I was w/kids who drinked-n-smoked ↑ and that meant I smoked too. I am *SCREWED*. I was like, Mom, why would u think that??? I would like to know that. She of course would not tell me. She was like, oh Marybeth, I hear that you and some friends think it's funny to go get stoned together like last wkend (which they were—stoned, but not me not really). I just ignored that comment. She's suspicious of *everything* I do these days.

Then she sat down and said we needed to have a long talk. But get this now I am not allowed out. And on top of that she decided that she really isn't talking to me. So I get the silent treatment and it's my job to unscramble her thoughts.

Billy

Ok so my stupid shlder I shouldn't be even typng with 1 hand. The doctor says I hav to kp in a lsing for 3–4 wks and the worst thing is no lacross for 4 weeks *FOUR WKS*!!! This is, besides a pain in th ass of me & evreyone, this is just *SAD* bc I wanted so much frm lacrosse thisyr. Today the doctor put on a bandage & he sez I have to lv it on for at lst 72 hours no dri ving no nothing and def. no lacross e I am so sad bout this I was frkkng out but now I have to take deep breath & may be it will go fat—how m,ch can i write like j=st hard & im typing fast as can???

gotta runnn hockey games on

Teresa

Jan 31

Dear Diary,

Last night Dad and I went to the JFK hockey tourney @ Brigg Valley, which is like an hour away. It was a matchup against the Bombers, another team I sorta like. And some of my other friends are actually team managers like what Emma does and what I secretly now want to do. Why would I turn down an opportunity to be around all those awesome & cute hockey players? I wouldn't!

So I sat w/my manager friends and soon after we'd been hanging there for a little while these 4 girls from the school came by real casual and sat near us. They were whispering. Whatever, I didn't really care. But then one of them says, "Who does she think she is?" and she was looking right at me with this look of total disgust, and I was so—well, I was really shocked. I was so mad at that moment that I stood up and looked right in her direction & said, "Excuse me, you fucking b*tch!?" But she was so busy whispering still she didn't even hear me!! At that point my dad figured out I was mad and he didn't want me to say anything else because I think he was afraid a fight would break out or we'd get kicked out or something.

Then I couldn't believe it after the game me & my dad were leaving and I actually heard someone go, "There she is." And someone else said, "Look, she has Daddy to protect her," and they were laughing at me. At me!! Well that was it totally. I just lost it. I went over to that stupid girl and got all in her face and said, "What are you talking about b*tch? Who won the f*cking game, huh?" Oh my God they so flipped out. They were surprised and then the girls started threatening to rip my hair out by the roots and my dad grabbed me away and this one fat guy was cursing me out and then my dad screamed that they should all watch their mouths.

When Daddy and I got into the car I really feel like I had accomplished something. I usually *NEVER* open my mouth in those situations. I never stick up for myself even at times when maybe I think someone is dissing me in public or wherever. But I finally *DID*!

I just don't understand what special thing I did that they felt this need to single me out of such a huge crowd. That is why I get paranoid walking in crowded rooms. I have really really *REALLY* bad luck in those situations.

Sometimes I wish soooo much that I were a little girl again, so I didn't have to deal with growing up. Isn't that wishful thinking? I know I am supposed to be responsible and everything, but it's *hard* to not just go ask my dad for help when I need some help.

p.s. Tonite is the Super Bowl but I'm not doing anything.

p.p.s. This is another new poem.

THE PAST LOOKING IN

I turn the pages in a book
And see photos that show my past.
Wet tears are in my eyes
And I think time just goes by too fast.

I always think
Of times that I had
A kiss from Mom
An embrace from Dad.

I turn the book's pages one by one
I want to see what joy it can bring.

A picture of me as a baby catches my eye
And there is my brother pretending to be king.

It makes me sad, very sad
Thinking of childhood gone.
There is no safety net to catch me fall
I have to face my own demons alone.

I very often miss the time
When I was protected all those years.
But never once do I regret
Needing protection from my fears.

Why can't I be young again?
I am growing older by the minute.
I was a kid for such a brief time
I barely felt like I was in it.

Now that I am becoming adult
I suppose I will see new things.
I will stay strong and beat my foes
Alone with all that brings.

—T. J. F. 1/30

Jake

January 31

There are some good things happening and man is it about time. Ok last night Micky Geffen and DJ Jonny came during the day because I had to stay home all day with my dad in case he needed something. I ordered a pizza and they ate over with me. Then my mom came home. She was at gymnastics with my little sister Jill. Jill is getting really good like scouts are even looking at her. My mom still wants her to be able to have lessons. So Geffen, Jon, and me went to Starbucks across town and just hung out. I drank hot chocolate with whipped cream in this cool mug. Then we went to Lazlo's to shoot pool.

Later on it was the Super Bowl and we went back to Lazlo's place to watch it on his big-screen TV. Yes the Broncos won for the second time in a row. It was good. We ate more pizza and chips. Just being with the guys was good.

Kevin

1/31

Super Bowl Sunday he he yesterday ohhh wait no it was Friday when Jonny got me sooo drunk I don't even recall most of what happened but oh well I do know it was mad phun!!! Yessssssss!

Nothing much happened Sat. but then last nite me and all of the usual people went down to the theater to grab tickets for *She's All That* and we had to wait like a half hour for May to get ready and then by the time we were at the tickets it was sold out ok but whatever like I'm over that already. So instead of movies we just shopped and then went back to go to Micky's (Lazlo) house. It was a dull yet funny nite. When I got home later I went online and I started talking to this ex of mine, Rosie, I've written about her before yeah like we went out for only 1 month last year at this time. Well she was really more like a friend w/benefits. Anyway we are still friends & we were talking online this nite. I realized talking to her that she is like really really hard to get over. I still say she kinda broke my heart a little bit. And I still really like her + would go out w/her again but we'll see what happens yeessss b/c when we were online she was talkin to me in this really cool way like leaving it open so maybe we could try & hook up again—well I was really really surprised about that. Like I told Rosie I was sorta flying solo now and then I said how maybe I had a thing for Cristina.

It was a good convo b/c basically she was saying Cris is not really a one-guy kinda person and I was better off just stayin friends w/her. She sez she's sick of all the guys @ our school (except me of course ha ha) and I agreed there are like no women to go for either b/c they're all hoochies like girls who have been around and who smoke and shit. Anyway I think then she was saying how she always ends up w/short guys and I was like, "I'm tall!" and she laughed. She was saying she wishes she could fall in love but I was like, "What are you talkin about you are sooo great gorgeous smart and everything and isn't everyone after you?" She said no way. I miss Rosie lots. She says she can trust me & talk w/me about a lot of shit, but she didn't go into much more than that. She was actually getting her driver's permit the next morning sooo she had to go very soon 4 beauty rest natch. We said good nite then & I was thinking she & I would be good together if only . . . Ta ta

Katie

January 31
@ 11:57 P.M.

A true friend is someone who lifts you up when your wings have trouble remembering how to fly.

↑ This quote reminds me of Gwen for some reason.

Tonite we came back from the beach, after months of not having been there. Me, Gwen, and my mom went away for the day to check our summer place there. It was so nice relaxing and reliving old memories. I can't *WAIT* to go back!!! Brad came over later when we got back.

By the way, Brad's family has been going crazy with everything that happened with Karl and Cindy. It is so awful what happened to her dad. I hope their trip back to Switzerland is okay. It is such an awful thing to have happened.

p.s. Rehearsals for *The Boy Friend* really get going more this month!!

Baxter

February 1

This is the best thing: There are only 26 days left until I, Edward Baxter, get my license. This is a major accomplishment, getting me in a car. Ha! Ha!

The day before yesterday was the Super Bowl. I went to my cousin's house for a while and watched it. My entire family was there. We had a lot of laughs. The food was great. Of course, my aunt Joan makes the best chicken wings ever. And I won $50.

Tomorrow will be hell. Hell = physics. So far physics is the #1 scariest thing about being a junior.

Emma

Right now my mom is shouting @ my little brother Ronnie because once again he has not done his homework, not that first graders get that much homework. She does that sometimes when she gets frustrated but I can understand why.

I am starting my SAT review class soon and that is a very bad thing. Well we get homework and they check it. I haven't done the math questions and barely finished the verbal section. I called Sherelle and Betsy to see if they remembered the math assignment and they said no too. I guess I will just do nothing and hope for the best. I can say I forgot. Actually, I heard that it was 3 1/2 hours for the whole class with half focused on verbal and half on the math. But I think we maybe get a bagel break. I mean, there are some good things about the class like my friends are mostly in it and also the teachers are really nice too.

Okay a big thing that happened was that I dreamed about getting my license, which is actually only 2 days away. I am still really, really scared. And dreams make me even more nervous. I keep asking my friends and they keep reassuring me but I just can't stop thinking it. Meanwhile on Sunday my dad took me to practice my parallel parking in this cool old drive-in lot. We practiced for a while—like 2 hours. I'm really really really really NERVOUS!!! xox, Emma

   p.s. Don't forget to get Cliff V-Day gift at the mall.
   (I wonder what he's getting me for my birthday?)

Jake

February 1
   Well no big surprises that my life totally sux. This year is the worst year ever, and everything continues to go downhill. Not one single thing can improve and my dad is actually getting worse. Now we have to buy a van so we can get him from place to place because there's nothing he can do. Only a van will accommodate his wheelchair.

   I lost the only girl that I ever truly had real feelings for. I loved Claudia so much and now she is gone.

   My friends don't tell me as much as they used to tell me. I even lost Kevin for a while when he was dating Adina in October because I barely ever saw him.

   Micky Lazlo never comes out anymore like he used to.

   Mick Geffen hangs out w/his girl rather than go out and Jonny is starting to talk to this girl that I was talking to the other nite Angie and so now I have nothing.

   My grades are slowly going down and I failed my HSPTs like I said so that now I have to be in this basic skills class. The more I think about that the worse I feel. I will be sitting with all the losers.

So then everything is going slowly downhill. I don't know what to do. All the women I want have boyfriends.

Teresa

Feb 2 (very very early the wee hours!)

Dear Diary,

Soooo it's a new month, which means that I have a new beginning. Thank God because I *definitely* need something new. Okay. This horoscope is *very* cool b/c I think it makes me think a lot about stuff.

> **Look alive, Libra. Go out on a limb and let your ideas blossom in the light! There's a planetary pileup in your house of creativity, drama, and romance. Your flair for the stage lights will be coming out too—or you may just show off a lot. One thing is certain: You seem to be meeting new guys wherever you go.**

I'm thinking . . . *WOW!* This really could be a good month as opposed to other ones esp. if the boy part of it comes true. So far this year Zach, Leonardo, Rusty, Hammy, Lawrence, or Kevin—none have been Mr. Right. But that's okay—I'm still trying to find him! Another *sign*!!!??? Sometimes I see the same things in different guys and this makes me think that I am looking for the "right one" in the wrong person sometimes. Does that make any sense? I can't explain myself very well when it comes to this subject. Maybe I don't know what I want after all. I mean all the good guys are either taken or they're gay and they don't want me ha ha ha!!!!

The only good thing here is that at least it's better than LAST year, which was the worst experience of my life really. I mean when I was a sophomore socially, it was the equivalent to being closed in a room alone for the rest of my life. Okay maybe it wasn't that bad, but it was pretty bad. The thing that was the biggest deal for me last year of course with guys and parents and all that was counseling (psychologist *not* a psychiatrist). No one really knows why I went. I had an anger issue but no one knew it. It had to do with friends' issues, and some about guys and people screwing me around. I basically had a lot of anxiety problems in like the springtime of sophomore year. Unfortunately something screwed up w/the insurance but that was fixed.

And last year I also just didn't seem to have boyfriends very often for whatever reason. Last year was pretty much just guys that I was talking to/w no real hookups. It was like a guy drought—until of course, I got carried away and would start liking someone more than they liked me—that was not a good thing. It was like no matter what I did nothing worked out like one guy I thought had some potential but then he started saying that he never would ever break up w/me like I was perfect or something and I was like *SLOW DOWN!!!* So I got scared and once again it's just striking out. Who knows what it means for me either back then or now. I just keep smiling because it has to work out somehow. Maybe this year I will get a rose for Valentine's Day. Okay I have written enough.

Romance Romance

<u>Billy:</u>

I'm not too romantic, not right now anyhow. I'm into parties and dif. girls, girls, girls. Maybe I'd like someone special but I don't know. Haven't met her yet.

<u>Teresa:</u>

1. I want a guy who is affectionate because actions speak louder than words.

2. I want a guy who has to want to be with me and only me.

3. I need someone who I can look up to as a security blanket.

4. I have to find someone who can accept my "deep" feelings about things and take a break occasionally from the intimate stuff.

5. I want a guy I can say anything to who will be my best friend too.

6. I want someone to say I LOVE YOU.

7. I want to have the kind of bond where you can go out to a really nice place one nite and then

159

the next just sit around and watch a movie and do nothing.

8. I want a guy who will do cute things like surprise me and like make stuff for me (he doesn't have to spend a lot of money or anything!).

9. I want someone who isn't afraid to show his emotion. You don't have to be a girl to cry!

10. I want to experience that feeling that everyone says you feel like in your toes. I want to know what that is like — being and falling in love for real. It's killing me!!!

Baxter:

I pick up Megan and bring her flowers. Then we go to a nice place for dinner, maybe this local restaurant Emilio's because it's dark there. Then we order dinner and hold hands. Later we just hang out and maybe see a movie. We kiss good night, a long kiss. That's how I would be romantic.

Romance Romance

Marybeth:

It means a lot 2 me being cared for when someone looks forward 2 seeing me or spending time w/me no matter what else is goin on. THAT gesture alone is the romantic part, I think u can get carried away on that. This Goo Goo Dolls song sums it up 4 me:

I'll do anything you ever dreamed to be complete
Little pieces of nothing that fall
Oh may
Put your arms around me

Kevin:

OK so there are like 5000 many freakin things that can make or break a romance like I should know. I think sweet romance is all these and much much more ok watching a sunset, back rubs, whispering, holdin her close w/my hands like on her back sometimes under her shirt mmm or buying each other gifts just because, when she wears my tuff tee or my

RomanceRomance

bracelets, writing poetry, saying I love you & she knows exactly what u mean by it, falling asleep together but like just bein close not w/sex, spending all ur time hangin together, flirting in school, staring at her eyes, smelling her hair, which smells like strawberries, when she sits on my lap, talking about dreams and shit, seein a romantic movie together and holding each other during the good parts (vs. seeing a romantic movie alone, which sux), driving around and then just stopping somewhere, saying the right thing so she gets all teary, talking Spanish or some other language, writing love notes, saying good nite and sweet dreams when you finish a date or whatever, and most of all I think it's romantic + a lot when you back her up if someone ever talks trash about your woman. Standing up for someone is like the most romantic thing you can do esp. if you have like tons of pressure to back down. You look so

RomanceRomance

good And you feel soooo Awesome like
you cAn sAy & know the right wAy
to be yeAh.

Katie:
   Romance is definitely Valentine's Day!
The thing is—I have always had a curse
around for Valentine's Day & never
thought I could find someone I'd be
with!!! And now Brad is here!!! I know
he will get me red roses, which is very
sweet and thoughtful. Being with him is
always romantic. We like it that way!

Jake:
   When you can have the best
conversations on the phone or you get
together and can't keep your hands off
her. Sometimes I like to get romantic
because then we hook up. That's only
sometimes like when I have been alone
for a while and I need it.

Emma:
   I dunno what romance is it depends. I

want someone who will listen because then that means he is really paying attention. Of course, for me I like to be the center of attention w/Cliff or get flowers maybe. I really think Cliff and me have a totally romantic relationship like when I got him those Taz boxers or he beeped me 143. Romance is when you know just the right thing to do or say.

Billy

Ok my shoulder is better and I am getting better at typing now too. Practice, practice, practice. I have to do my homewrk on this computer and it takes forever and ever. Right now I am working on therapy w/my shoulder with this Doctor Burges so it is ok feeling. He says def. no fracture on there. He told me if it hrts I should pack in ice + relax. He was the one who had to pop it back into place, which was a little hard. rjght now his main concern is getting back a range of motion inmy arms and sholder. It really sucks to miss lacrosse but Jake says practices aren't really geared up yet. I'll deal with it. I have to work at this Dad says. It's a 2–3 week recovry w/work on weights and other machines to take care of the problem. More L8er . . .

Baxter

February 3

Well, I was right. My real problem was my physics midterm. It was impossible. I studied for 3 hours and got a B-. He said that that was a little above the average but I'm not happy with it. Today we had another test on finding the pressure of a fluid on a block and pressure due to atmosphere. I think I did really good, which makes me feel a little bit better.

Later on today things were ok until someone stole 3 candy bars from me! We were selling them for the senior center. This is the second box I would have sold and now it's gone. Why would someone do this to me? I hope they're happy.

Megan hasn't beeped in days. She is just being the biggest *BITCH* to me. She is sooo moody I just don't understand. I have decided that I don't like her anymore. I think I'm back to liking Jessica again. I see her more anyway.

Tonight turned out better because I went out with Emma for her birthday. We had a great time. I am so happy that she passed her driving test because she was so nervous about it. She made me nervous!

The only thing was that I felt bad about not getting her a gift. I totally spaced on getting the gift. I didn't want her to know so I made up something. I just thought she would have a family birthday party like she always does but she didn't.

We went out to the Silverado with Marybeth, Sherelle, Betsy Geffen, and of course Cliff and some other people. They all got her stuff but she didn't care though. We had ice cream and french fries and a lot of laughs. I can't believe Emma is 17.

I PASSED!!   2/3, 7:20 p.m.
Happy birthday to me!

Okay Cliff got me a Tommy Hilfiger sweater and two pairs of supersoft socks and a T-shirt I wanted from Abercrombie & Fitch. He forgot and left on the tags and now I know he really spent a lot of money on me. And all the clothes are really really cute. I am going to wear this all the time. Also Cliff's mom Peg sent me flowers. When I came home from school I saw that I had 2 deliveries in my room! I opened the card and saw they were from her. I was so shocked that I almost cried. Marybeth knew but she never said anything to me. Cliff had asked for my home address from her because he didn't know it for the florist. I have to send her a thank-you card right away. I'd call her now but she's at work.

Tonite I went to the Silverado for a hamburger and to be with everyone and celebrate my 17th birthday. A bunch of us went including Baxter and Marybeth, Betsy, Karen, Sherelle, and Cliff. I got some cute gifts from all my friends. MB got me a gift certificate to Banana Republic and a copy of *Chicken Soup for the Teenage Soul 2,* which I really really wanted but could never find it. Sherelle got me a gift certificate to Contempo Casuals so I would get my own shoes (I'm always borrowing hers!). Karen got me a gift certificate too—to the place where I get my nails done. That made me excited because I didn't think she was going to get me anything. Baxter said he has my present at home and he'll get it to me later. I think he got me a stuffed animal or something maybe—he always remembers what I like. Betsy gave me a yellow rose and these teddy bear balloons, which were cute. My little brother Ronnie loves them they're actually in his room right now. Katie couldn't come to dinner but she got me a picture frame. I have to put a picture of her and me into it. Everyone else in my family got me money except my aunt, who is going to give me this family ring. I think it has diamonds in it. I plan to wear it *every day* to school.

I just can't believe I have my license now. It is really weird, especially after all that worrying. Like now my mom doesn't have to be in the car with me anymore. My parents are already being a little strict about me driving places but I know that is just because it's new for them too. Whatever they'll figure it out. Today after I got my license I dropped off my mom here and then pulled away. That was the weird part, it was sooo strange to do that and have her watching me pull away. It's such a weird feeling that I can't explain. Now I know how Kevin feels.

I love Cliff so much!

Teresa

Feb 4 (12:00 am)

Dear Diary,

Emma got her license. I'm really happy for her. I actually have been thinking how I miss her a lot lately. We used to be a lot closer than we are now and I want to be that way again. I wonder what happened.

Me and my other girlfriends were talking today how our other friend Gina is kinda changing lately. All of a sudden it's like she doesn't want to hang out anymore. I dunno why everyone does this. First it was Stephanie and her bf and now Gina. It seems like this year more than ever before we're all moving in these different directions. It makes me sad inside. I mean, it's okay to want to find new friends but that's no reason to diss old ones, is it?

We all have to talk about this a lot more. Maybe this is why I feel like I should be connecting w/Emma. I don't know.

Kevin

Um I had a quick swim practice after school today so that was cool & there was also a pasta party for the swim team from 6:00 to 8:00 to get carbs for tomorrow's regional match, which could be an interesting event. Of course I won't be there b/c of life guarding and all that but that's ok w/me. Tonite I hung w/Jonny, Jake, Micky G., Sherelle, Suzie, Rebecca Rinaldi, Marybeth, Emma, and Randi it was like the whole crew but the night basically sucked though it was shitty boring and annoying. We went to Lazlo's but ohhh well what can you do. I have to study for a life-guarding test coming up -n- I swear I will fail!

p.s. Last nite I talked real quick to Rosie on the computer and nothing spectacular happened but we said again the stuff about getting together and how we liked each other and now maybe we'll chill out tomorrow or something maybe but that's it. Ta ta

Marybeth

February 5th

Well it's not scary but I am still a little freaked lately about the fact that we r all growing ↑. Emma had her b-day get-together and I can't believe *she* is

170

17—how wild! Pretty soon we'll be "legal" age & the stupid things we do 4 fun now could get us into serious trouble then b/c we'd be "adults." Stupid jokes would be taken the wrong way I know it. Like right now we r being "prepared" 4 life or whatever by those around us, but I think the real world is a tough place & how can u b sure that u r doin the right thing and livin in the right place? How can u know that ur satisfied? I never feel that way. Like I think it's scary to try right now to figure out what I want 2 do w/the rest of my life. I have *NO* idea.

Ok I found this funny ha ha thing online & I just had to save it. B/c of course I am a baby of the 80s. Ok this is funny—and so true!!

<u>You</u> <u>Know</u> <u>You're</u> <u>a</u> <u>Child</u> <u>of</u> <u>the</u> <u>1980s</u> . . .

You had a crush on someone in New Kids on the Block or Menudo.

You wanted to be on *Star Search.*

You played Pong on Atari.

You knew the profound meaning of "Wax on. Wax off."

You hold a special place in your heart for *Back to the Future.*

You wore a banana clip or slouch socks and puff painted at least one shirt.

You knew how to break-dance and lambada.

You wondered why Smurfette was the only female Smurf.

171

You owned a Swatch watch.

You watched *Gummi Bears, Double Dare, My Little Pony,* or *Zoobilee Zoo.*

You own some of the Care Bears glass collection they gave out at Pizza Hut.

You carried an E.T. or Gremlins lunch box.

You watched hours of *Fraggle Rock* and then moved on to hours of *Saved by the Bell.*

Katie

February 5
@ 8:45 P.M.

Play practice is taking up so much time—it's been rough every day with double sessions every other day from 3 to 5 and 6 to 8. It's hell but I love it! Typical. Not much else has happened because I have been so focused on *The Boy Friend* and my schoolwork. Well, there was one (teeny) problem with Brad.

It's not really a problem, though. It's just that he told me he was a little upset because we don't see each other every day. I understand what he is saying and where he is coming from. My friends and his friends see each other at school and whatnot. But it just isn't possible for Brad and me to do the same because our schedules conflict and our lifestyles are different. I love Brad more than anything, and I would love to spend every second with him, but I've just learned to accept the fact that I can't.

Anyway, so what happened after he got upset about it was that I cried. Then he cried. And then I fell down onto the floor, just sort of collapsed and that really started me crying more. But we resolved everything. Everything is fine now.

Jake

February 5

Well tonite I went out with Jonny and we picked up Rebecca Rinaldi to go to a basketball game at Grimes. It was a girls' game and JFK lost by *a lot*. Then we went to May's after driving around and chilled for a little bit. We hit like 100 mph in Jonny's car on the way over to May's and Rebecca was getting scared. But she got over it and we got there. Then Kevin and Micky met up with us, but I really didn't want Kevin to be there because he's been kind of an asshole lately. Jonny is mad at him too. Then we went to the Silverado to eat and later over to Lazlo's to chill some more. They were all being dicks and wanted to leave at only 11:00 so me and Jonny, Micky and Rebecca left and went and got Micky Geffen. All we did was drive around pointlessly and then go home. Basically it really sucked because I was supposed to chill with Rebecca Rinaldi for a while all to myself tonight. Meanwhile I'm left with nothing to do.

Billy

My mom and dad took me to Staples this afternoon & we got a new mouse. I've been on my computer ever since. I've been thinking about Valentine's Day coming up soon. I think I've changed my mind. I *DO* want a valentine. There are a few poss. girls @ JFK but anything is possible to happen or not happen. Esp. with a busted shoulder.

I have to use the computer for evrything now. The funny part is I can't always spell and get it right. My teachers are laughing at some of the spelling mistakes but they won't penalize me. They feel bad. Tonite Lee called to see how I was doing. He was worried about me, which is nice. I have to go for therapy this afternoon.

Marybeth

February 6th

My mom and dad went pretty nutz on me today. This is like a regular thing these dayz. Ok so I wuz w/kids last nite that were smoking (some from The Mix) and someone *saw me* w/them (one of my mom's friends I think). Now *again* she thinks I was doin stuff too but *I WASN'T!!!*

She was telling me that I didn't make the best choices and told me that "cigarettes are the gateway drug." I laughed b/c that just sounds like what *everyone* says. I tried 2 tell her that just b/c I hang w/them (meaning The Mix) doesn't mean I smoke & am guilty. But she said I look it. Guilt by association I think. She was mad & kept telling me I wuz missing the pt. Then she started saying how all 3 things (alcohol, drugs, & sex) all go together and if I do one I'll do the other 2. Meanwhile Daddy was sitting there with this mean-ass look on his face saying how it would be a VERY long summer if he ever found out I wuz lying to him & Mom.

Now yes most parties I go to lately have drinking this is true & yes sometimes I drink, like rum or Everclear or daiquiris. But this is clear——Mommy knows about the drinking b/c if I ever think I will be drinking *anything* I tell her. Her biggest rule other than watch my back and keep my wits about me is that I am just not allowed to come home drunk NOT EVER. But well, we fight about this. I guess she doesn't know what really goes on @ the parties, which is like pretty normal stuff, playing cards and hanging out nothing major. Ok sometimes 4 fun there r drinking games & one party (that was sooooo BAD) had like everyone in a dif. room or shower giving BJs or having sex. That was not my scene. I am really not getting into trouble. Why doesn't she just trust me & give me a chance? Most parties end up mellow.

It really sux that they think I am out there drinking, having sex, and doing drugs. Mommy said she rarely believes me when I say where I am going 2 go. I thought gee this is great nobody trusts me. And what sux even worse is that *I DO TELL THE TRUTH*. So now it doesn't even matter b/c whether I lie or not they still won't believe me. I dunno. I am so anxious about what I am gonna do—but I sure know that one mess up & I am toast.

Stress Stress Stress

Katie:
    With AP classes, Community Club, Brad, SATs, etc., I expected this year to be one of the most stressful of my life thus far. . . . I have discovered, though, that I can handle a ton of responsibilities and still get good results. I expected to be a nutcase this year, but in contrast, I have had a relatively stress free time. I just remember a book Dad got for me going into this year called Don't Sweat the Small Stuff (and It's All Small Stuff). I have followed that and found success focusing on the larger picture.

Jake:
    I won't let anxiety get me. I have too much to do first for me and for my dad.

Emma:
    I dunno really what "anxiety" is and the truth is with school I don't always deal well with stress I hate being put under pressure and I hate when teachers

give tests all on the same day. . . . That makes me nuts and sometimes I get all nervous and I hate it because like I'll shake and then my stomach will hurt and I just hate that feeling.

Billy:

Anxiety = getting bad grades & then facing my dad w/the news.

Teresa:

Oh boy! Bad memories. Back during my sophomore year, when I was seeing a counselor, one of the first things he told me was that I had an anxiety problem. I had to explain what happened when I got nervous. So I told him how my shoulders crunch up and I get hot and twitch a body part. He said that that was my main problem . . . anxiety. The problem is that I put too much pressure on myself. I'm an overachiever so I'm always hoping to do more than I need to in some way. So

178

Stress Stress Stress

basically I'm always under stress. I really don't know how to relax. Next week I'm going if I can get away to a seminar on how to enjoy life! As of right now, I haven't had much anxiety in my life besides the basic everyday stress (homework, guys, etc.). Let's keep it that way!!!!

Baxter:

This year I have become less nervous & anxious. When you have Mr. MacTaggart for chem you have to be. In that class you learn to roll with it. No matter what happens during class you mark higher usually.

marybeth:

When it feels like no one likes me or trusts me I get anxious. I usually say that I'm upset or something 4 nothing.

Kevin:

He he he . . . um I hAve worRY And Am Anxious About A lot of

Stress Stress Stress

things, whether I am making good
decisions to what I want in life,
if I'll get out of life what I
want and dream of. I get all
anxious about the health of all my
loved ones so that nothing will
happen to them. I would really
be upset if anything did happen.
It's just that I am worried soooo
about getting in an accident with
my car I really don't want to
get hurt first of all and second
I don't want to screw up my car
that I put a lot into. I guess
that's it.

Baxter

February 6

Yesterday I went to the boys' basketball game w/Megan. Ok so I know I wanted to forget all about her but I didn't and couldn't. We went to the game just the two of us too, which I never would have imagined happening after all that has (*NOT*) happened between us.

Then after the game we walked around and I offered her some ice cream and my jacket too. But she wouldn't take either. We talked forever and then walked back to my house finally. We talked the whole way home. It was a long walk. I was in disbelief about it while it was happening, especially since I was like *THIS CLOSE* to giving up on her. I had even unmemorized her beeper number ha ha.

Then when we got to my place, I showed her inside the house and she met my parents. My mom drove her home afterward.

I fell right back in love with her.

♥ I LOVE MEGAN!!!

Teresa

Dear Diary,

A few things to clarify:

- Boys are nonexistent right now and I am pissed about that.
- Family life is great except for never talking to Vin my older brother.
- Friends are ok.
- Work is *GREAT!!!! I LOVE KIDS SO MUCH!!!*
- Life is good.

Tonite I am going to stay over at college w/Jaclyn Roome. My dad is driving me up there. She graduated last year and she is like a sister to me sometimes. I know she's close w/Katie too. I cannot wait to see her. I've never been to her place. *PLUS* she told me that some guy found a picture of me in her dorm room and said, "She is so hot!" So now Jaclyn wants to fix me up with the guy. We're gonna be hooked up tomorrow and I can't wait!

Okay to finish up, here's a poem I wrote this week (I still wanna change a few things and it doesn't have a name yet). Oh yeah, I have been thinking that maybe I should say something to Kevin about having this thing for him still. I don't know. Maybe I should give him this poem and see what happens!? Nooooo way!!!! Ha!

My heart softly weeps
This feeling is for keeps
As I see you walk in
Why is being with me a sin?

I saw that other girl's face
I wish I could be in her place
Does she know what she's got
Or does she love you not?

I may not be much better
I wish you would forget her
But only you can choose
And I am guessing that I lose.

Your smile makes my heart melt
L-O-V-E is what my heart spelled
Because of you I understood
All things a 16-year-old should.

Relationships are not dice
Being single isn't always nice
For you I would change all my ways
I still want you 24/7 for 365 days.

However I know this isn't going to be
For reasons that are unknown to me
But if maybe feelings ebb again
Know that my heart will soon return.

Maybe our timing is always wrong
Maybe fate says we shouldn't get along
So for now the door will briefly close
Without me is the life you chose.

Kevin

Today was pretty stressful b/c I had a chem test that I thought I had like totally failed—a midterm and then I had a swim meet and then this life-guarding test. So I was like really really stressed out and wasn't home much at all. So anyway I got a B on the chem test & then passed life guarding and then we lost the meet but ohhhh well. My life-guarding teacher is really cute. I could be w/her I think so more on that one maybe something could happen there like after practice or something I'll see yeah right.

Ok so the only thing that is going on outside of that is this freakin *MAJOR* problem I'm having w/Katie. It all goes to this convo when she told Sherelle something I said that we talked about in like total confidence & all. What this means is trust between friends was broken b/c of Katie. I cannot *BELIEVE* this happened & I swear now—see someone innocently asked me & Katie why Sher & Betsy don't talk and Katie sez, "Oh it's all Betsy's fault," and I'm like staring at her in disbelief b/c that is so not what happened *AT ALL* ok.

Ok ok back up what happened was that a long, long time ago last summer everyone said Sherelle was doin the unthinkable, which was hooking up with Betsy's bf on Mem Day weekend. And yeah she was really messing with his head. It was pretty f-ugly. Now I used to date Sherelle like a million yrs ago so I can say this knowing what she is like ok. She obviously chose at a certain point knowing some trouble would happen. Now b4 then, she was JUST friends with this guy, but then he was drinking one nite & so he kept pursuing and trying and asking her to do stuff first as a joke and then he blew off his own gf Betsy & tried to go out w/Sher. But of course she was stringing him & finally she gave him the cold shoulder & was just really mean to him. She had *NO* feelings for this guy—it was like the whole situation was a *TOTAL WASTE*. It was like some bullshit game.

Ok so no one understands how much this has hurt Betsy, I mean she was pissed off but much more she was crushed too. I mean not only did she lose her bf but she used to be friends w/Sherelle!!! Truth is that girl cried in my arms at least a dozen times in the past 6 months! Ok so now there's this huge division w/all of us like then we all started taking sides whether we wanna go w/Sher or Betsy.

Now I am still the best of friends with both of them and love them both to death cause I let them deal with their confrontations they're old enough to deal with it themselves and be left like that. I just think it was wrong for Katie to take sides esp. on the *wrong* side & I want her to know this and that I am upset about it, I don't know why it's bothering me those are her own reasons and I respect that.

p.s. Beyond all this the truth is that Sherelle is like a dif. person than she used to be and I don't understand anyone who can't see that.

Katie

February 9
@ 11:40 P.M.

The weirdest thing happened and it has driven this wedge bet. me and some other friends @ JFK. We were all driving someplace just last nite and for whatever reason the subject of Sherelle and Betsy came up. Those two don't speak since last year. They had an awful falling-out with their friendship. It was this awful boyfriend incident & I think they're rebuilding but I don't know for sure. I don't know why Kevin gets so upset when the whole episode gets mentioned. It's not like he was dating one of them.

Anyway I guess since I favor Sherelle's "side" in the argument, I have to admit that I come off sounding like I don't really like Betsy, which is not true. I mean, I think she might be wrong in this situation—that's all. But I made the mistake of saying that out loud. Well, obviously Kevin doesn't want to hear *that* or anything bad about his "Betsy" and then he starts yelling at me and then I couldn't help myself—I was crying. I felt so sad inside. I do not like to be yelled at. I think I've had to endure enough of that in my life. When people yell at me it triggers memories, like of Robert—esp. if that person happens to be a good friend. I get upset, and I try to talk it out.

So what did I do next that was so bad? I went to Sherelle to tell her that Kev & I had talked, etc. etc. This was of course a big mistake because Marybeth heard about it and went back to Kevin! And now this is the e-mail Kevin just sent to me:

I am going back on Marybeth who heard what you said this weekend. She told me how you were telling Sherelle that you & I had a fight and disagreement over the whole situation w/her & Betsy. What happened was not for Sher or Betsy to hear no one is supposed to be told about what we talk about privately. That's the deal I just don't know if I could trust you do I have to watch what I say now since things will get out and affect what goes on with all this shit. I do think it was wrong for you to bring this up of course. I don't hate you for it I just want you to know this and that I am upset very upset. So what do we do now?

Marybeth

February 9th

Ok I love her to death, but yesterday Katie seriously needed to be smacked. For whatever reason a group of us were together and for some reason the topic came up about Sherelle & Betsy and how they hate each other sometimes. The thing is that Katie started talking all over the place as if somehow whatever happened had been Betsy's fault alone. The fact is that is no way true, not at all. Sherelle was the instigator on this whole bf-stealing thing w/Betsy, to get attention and get whatever she wanted. Even tho she's my friend, I don't agree w/how she handles herself a lot of the time. She was a little bitchy here 4 sure.

Anyway, Katie actually told Sherelle about how Kevin thinks. And it didn't stop there. Then she went and told something to Emma too, but Em had already heard it. I hope all this *BULLSHIT* just stops right here.

Emma

2/10, 7:45 p.m.

Things have been weird since I got my license. I feel so strange getting into the car and just going when I want. Cliff loves the fact that I can drive. I actually took him to work yesterday because his brother forgot to pick him up. What he did was beep me with 1027-911, which is call me right back. So I did and then he was like, "Can you give me a ride," and I was like ok. It was a good chance to see him as a surprise and he looked soo cute in his work uniform. Right when I dropped him off too, he leaned over and kissed me it was cute. I always told him I could take him to work if he had no ride but I just didn't expect him to really call. He doesn't want me to feel obligated in any way so I'll just roll with it.

Teresa

Feb 11

Dear Diary,

Last weekend I went to see Jaclyn. And *that* was a lotta fun! Ok when I first pulled up to the school w/my dad I felt as if I were going there myself for real-life college and it was *SCARY*. I got this wave of mixed-up emotions all at the same time like anxiety, fear, nerves, excitement, and anticipation. I wonder if this is how I will feel on my first day when the *real* day comes.

Anyway, Jaclyn's suite was nice and big. She actually has 5 other roommates. I ended up meeting her guy friends from across the hall and we totally hit it off right away. I ended up hitting it off best w/this guy Charles and we told Jaclyn how we felt too but then ended up blowing it off. He is about to turn 21. I mean, that's not too bad. Needless to say, I raved about him when I got home—and apparently Jaclyn said he did the same. Hmmm . . .

Anyway later on that nite I met Jaclyn's bf and his *HOT* friends. All of them are from a town right near JFK and so we talked about the neighborhood and some mutual friends and families, which was cool. Then I got introduced to this guy Timothy and I swear he is *THE CUTEST GUY I EVER MET!* I was in love with him instantly. It is a huge, huge crush for sure. And here's the good news. Jaclyn called me today to say that Timothy said he would definitely hook up w/me so I should come back real soon!!! Long story short—I am heading back there on the 27th with my BFF Wendy. I made a plan right away just in case. Wendy gets her license on the 22nd and so she can drive us up. I cannot wait!!!

p.s. We had this thing for Community Club where we match up percentages and find our perfect partner. It sounds corny, but you plug in all your answers and it prints out compatibility percentages. Here's the really funny part, which is my best match for both my entire school and w/in my grade—*BAXTER*!!? How funny is that? Katie did the match too and her #1 match was Kevin ☺ .

What's that about? The good thing is that Kevin made it on my list at #3. That made me smile.

p.p.s. Still no real valentine!

 My broken heart

Baxter

February 12

Tonight there was this party at this girl's house who's friends with my buddy Derek. She was having the party supposedly just for juniors. Well, it wound up being seniors and even people who graduated before that. There was sooooo much smoke in the place that I felt like my eyes were about to pop out of my sockets.

The really big thing that happened at the party was that Billy and some of his friends from the team were there. They tried to hold me down and make me drink. They were pouring beer into my mouth. It wound up all over my face. I was so *PISSED OFF*. I just stormed out of the room and cursed everyone off. I hate that. I was so mad. I just don't know what came over me. I called my dad to come get me and then I left.

Billy

Last nite there was this big-ass drinking party and it was *AMAZING*. It was madd women and madd beer is all I can say. I was drinking some Jack Daniels and OJ. It's so good. Baxter was around but he wouldn't try anything—no fun! My arm was still hurting me tonight but I went anyhow.

At the party, this girl Olivia was flirting like crazy w/me. Now I know her a little from before. We were in Fla. once for chorus together and ended up talking all the way around on the bus. At the party we were sitting there without really moving for like 2 hours straight. From then on I have wanted her like crazy.

So here she was at this party and Olivia was flirting and she was also drunk. B/c of that she was like caressing my legs and back and shit. It felt real nice though but I didn't know what to do b/c she has a boyfriend.

Kevin

2/13

I had work from 7–10:30 and it would have been boring if Renee wasn't there like it would be tolerable but boring. I like her and all we'll see if that goes somewhere for now it's Rosie on my mind. I called

Rosie on the phone for a little while today. After school we had the swim team pizza party and exchanged presents and all that and it set a much happier mood for the rest of the day. I met up w/Micky Lazlo and his girl and Rosie to go see *She's All That*. It was weird like not too good but after was great b/c we trekked over to May's place and b/c May's mom & dad are away we could have a party. No one was gonna drink so it was a little boring, but it was cool that me & Rosie ended up hooking up like the whole time. It was very cool. I forgot from before when we dated what a good kisser she was. She kisses sooo much better than Adina ever did.

Teresa

Feb 13

The worst thing happened today in school. Well, first of all everyone was in the Valentine's Day mood (those who have valentines of their own at least) so it started out sickening enough—and got worse!!

This girl Rosie who is in ALL of my classes started gabbing w/me in the morning and she hands me this card she found in her locker that was there along w/a bag of candy. I read the card and it said:

DeAr Rosie,
    I wAs wondeRing whAt you weRe

doing on V-DAY becAuse I couldn't think of spending V-DAY with Anyone else but you. I love you!

Kevin (MorAn)

Whoa when I read that my heart dropped. Now keep in mind she has *NO* idea of how I feel about Kevin obviously. But needless to say, I tried to sound as happy as I could for her. It was tough. I was nearly in tears for some reason. Then she told me that she and Kevin are kind of "talking" and that crushed me even more.

Valentine's Day always brings back some bad memories for me. Last year at this time I was dating this guy Nino, who was like the sweetest thing ever. But for some weird reason on V-Day he didn't even ask me to hang out. I had presents for him and he had presents for me too, but we just didn't spend time together. So then I did this very, very bad thing. I took all my anger I felt for him, went out to this nearby club, and I cheated on him w/this other guy. He still doesn't know I did that.

Since that day I have held a grudge against Valentine's Day and this year looks to be even worse. Okay maybe if I had someone in my life and love I wouldn't be so bitter, but since I don't I'll say whatever I want. Anyway, I should just go to bed now! I'm pretty tired.

Emma

Well right now me and Teresa are not speaking.
We haven't been talking for like a week already now.
On my birthday more than a week ago I was supposed to take her home from school. She had asked
me about it for like 2 days and I was also excited to
do it since I could finally drive places. Well when we
were going to get into my car, we saw this guy our
friend Jonny walking to his car. He likes Teresa and
she likes him and he also has a really nice car. And he
said come on, Teresa, let me take you home. I was
like no way Jonny I'm taking her home, but he kept it
up. And she went w/him! She fucking went with
HIM! I told her right there that she could never step
foot in my car from that moment on. Everyone knows
how much it pissed me off and they know she is
wrong. And she just goes into denial about these
things, like they never happened I swear. All she has
to say to me is I'm sorry and then it'll be ok again but
she won't even do that much. Whatever. Until she
says that, I am not talking to her.

Katie

I talked to Kevin again today about the whole Sherelle and Betsy mess. I am still so upset about what happened. And when he sent me that e-mail it made me more upset than before. I e-mailed him back just now for the tenth time to say that I can't stop thinking about it and how much it bothers me what I did and how I never wanted to betray his trust or anyone's trust in the group. I guess in the end it's not a huge deal but we are apologizing anyway.

Wow, I hate high school so much right about now. I am trapped in this world and place—I don't want to be trapped. I need to get away from all this. I just am having one of those moments where I feel like everyone around me is fake. I can't stand that feeling. I hate it. As much as I love all my friends, I need a change so badly.

Jake

February 13
Today I stayed in bed until real late because I was feeling a little sick. Then I went looking for vans with my parents for my dad. We found a few but didn't buy any yet. Then we came back toward home and decided

to go get pizzas for dinner. So we stopped off at Vito's our used-to-be hangout after school. And I waited there for the pizza. The owner started talking to me because he knows me a little and he is a very nice guy. And then he said to me, "I didn't know your dad had died." He misunderstood my mom when she told him that my dad was so sick and I corrected him and told him Dad was not dead.

At that point sooo many things ran through my head. I was ready to cry but I didn't. I didn't know what to think. My life just gets worse and worse day by day. I just wish this wouldn't happen to me. I would do anything.

Marybeth

February 13th

Life is so-so. TJ was supposed to come over & see me but he didn't. I'll have to screw w/him 4 that one. Other stuff going on: I got a surprise e-mail from my favorite person that kid Rick Wright. What is up with him anyway? Once again he proceeds to tell me what a bitch I am. He then claims that he doesn't care who I hook up with and meanwhile I know for a fact that he does—all the time. I was telling him about getting in deep shit w/my mom but he seemed not to care too much. He was pretty distant and weird overall. Who knows.

People have changed lately. The people who I could "read like a book" have totally changed. It's like we get so used to some things and then they shift to a new thing and it's so hard to deal with it. And @ home too, like w/ my mom & dad. The word *change* itself is even strange. Change isn't just about one moment and then another. It's this constant moving thing.

I think that junior year may be the biggest year of changes to date. The more things stay the same, the more they change. I see my friends and bfs all around and we're making these lifelong decisions here. Like where we want to spend all of our time and other significant adjustments. Wow I can't believe the year is already more than 1/2 way over. And we still have a long road ahead still b4 we figure it out it's flyin by!

"No matter where you go, there you are."

Real feelings. Real issues. Real life.

real teens

Diary of a Junior Year

VOLUME 5
COMING IN FEBRUARY

Teen.

RT499